THE PILGRIMS' WAY FROM WINCHESTER TO CANTERBURY

BY

JULIA CARTWRIGHT

JULIA CARTWRIGHT

CHAPTER I

THE PILGRIMS' WAY

THREE hundred and seventy years have passed since the shrine of St. Thomas at Canterbury was swept away, and the martyr's ashes were scattered to the winds. The age of pilgrimages has gone by, the conditions of life have changed, and the influences which drew such vast multitudes of men and women to worship at the murdered Archbishop's tomb have long ago ceased to work on the popular mind. No longer does the merry cavalcade of Chaucer's lay ride forth in the freshness of the spring morning, knight and merchant, scholar and lawyer, Prioress and Wife of Bath, yeoman and priest and friars, a motley company from all parts of the realm, "ready to wenden on their pilgrimage with full devout courage" to Canterbury. The days of pilgrimages are over, their fashion has passed away, but still some part of the route which the travellers took can be traced, and the road they trod still bears the name of the Pilgrims' Way. Over the Surrey hills and through her stately parks the dark yews which lined the path may yet be seen. By many a quiet Kentish homestead the grassy track still winds its way along the lonely hill-side overlooking the blue Weald, and, if you ask its name, the labourer who guides the plough, or the waggoner driving his team, will tell you that it is the Pilgrims' Road to Canterbury. So the old name lives, and the memory of that famous pilgrimage which Chaucer sang has not yet died out of the people's heart. And although strangers journey no longer from afar to the martyrs shrine, it is still a pleasant thing to ride out on a spring or summer morning and follow the Pilgrims' Way. For the scenes through which it leads are fair, and the memories that it wakes belong to the noblest pages of England's story.

In those old days the pilgrims who came to Canterbury approached the holy city by one of the three following routes. There was first of all the road taken by Chaucer's pilgrims from London, through Deptford,

Greenwich, Rochester, and Sittingbourne; the way trodden by all who came from the North, the Midlands, and the Eastern Counties, and by those foreigners who, like Erasmus, had first visited London. But the greater number of the foreign pilgrims from France, Germany, and Italy landed at Sandwich Haven or Dover, and approached Canterbury from the south; while others, especially those who came from Normandy and Brittany, landed at Southampton and travelled through the southern counties of Hampshire, Surrey, and Kent. Many of these doubtless stopped at Winchester, attracted by the fame of St. Swithun, the great healing Bishop; and either here or else at Guildford, they would be joined by the pilgrims from the West of England on their way to the Shrine of Canterbury. This was the route taken by Henry II. when, landing at Southampton on his return from France, he made his first memorable pilgrimage to the tomb of the murdered Archbishop, in the month of July, 1174. And this route it is, which, trodden by thousands of pilgrims during the next three centuries, may still be clearly defined through the greater part of its course, and which in Surrey and Kent bears the historic name of the Pilgrims' Way. A very ancient path it is, older far than the days of Plantagenets and Normans, of shrines and pilgrimages. For antiquarian researches have abundantly proved this road to be an old British track, which was in use even before the coming of the Romans. It may even have been, as some writers suppose, the road along which caravans of merchants brought their ingots of tin from Cornwall to be shipped at what was then the great harbour of Britain, the Rutupine Port, afterwards Sandwich Haven, and then borne overland to Massilia and the Mediterranean shores. Ingots of tin, buried it may be in haste by merchants attacked on their journey by robbers, have, it is said, been dug up at various places along this route, and British earthworks have been found in its immediate neighbourhood.

The road was, there can be no doubt, used by the Romans; and all along its course remains of Roman villas, baths, and pavements have been brought to light, together with large quantities of Roman coins, cinerary urns, and pottery of the most varied description. In mediæval days this "tin road," as Mr. Grant Allen calls it, still remained the principal thoroughfare from the West to the East of England. It followed the long line of hills which runs through the north of Hampshire, and across

Surrey and Kent, that famous chalk ridge which has for us so many different associations, with whose scenery William Cobbett, for instance, has made us all familiar in the story of his rides to and from the Wen. And it lay outside the great trackless and impassable forest of Anderida, which in those days still covered a great part of the south-east counties of England. Dean Stanley, in his eloquent account of the Canterbury pilgrimage, describes this road as a byway, and remarks that the pilgrims avoided the regular roads, "probably for the same reason as in the days of Shamgar, the son of Anath, the highways were unoccupied, and the traveller walked through byways." But the statement is misleading, and there can be little doubt that in the twelfth and thirteenth centuries this road was, if not the only means of communication between West and East, at least the principal thoroughfare across this part of England, and was as such the route naturally chosen by pilgrims to Canterbury.

Certain peculiarities, it is interesting to notice, mark its course from beginning to end. It clings to the hills, and, wherever it is possible, avoids the marshy ground of the valleys. It runs, not on the summit of the downs, but about half-way down the hill-side, where there is shelter from the wind, as well as sunshine to be had under the crest of the ridge. And its course is marked by rows of yew trees, often remarkable for their size and antiquity. Some of these are at least seven or eight hundred years old, and must have reared their ancient boughs on the hill-side before the feet of pilgrims ever trod these paths. So striking is this feature of the road, and so fixed is the idea that some connection exists between these yew trees and the Pilgrims' Way, that they are often said to have been planted with the express object of guiding travellers along the road to Canterbury. This, however, we need hardly say, is a fallacy. Yews are by no means peculiar to the Pilgrims' Way, but are to be found along every road in chalk districts. They spring up in every old hedgerow on this soil, and are for the most part sown by the birds. But the presence of these venerable and picturesque forms does lend an undeniable charm to the ancient track. And in some places where the line of cultivation gradually spreading upwards has blotted out every other trace of the road, where the ploughshare has upturned the sod, and the hedgerows have disappeared, three or four of these grand old trees may still be seen standing by themselves in the midst of a ploughed field, the last relics of a bygone age.

The murder of Becket took place on the 29th of December, 1170. At five o'clock on that winter evening, as the Archbishop was on his way to vespers, the King's men, Reginald Fitz Urse and three knights who had accompanied him from Saltwood Castle, rushed upon him with their swords and murdered him in the north transept of his own Cathedral. The tragic circumstance of Becket's end made a profound impression on the people of England, and universal horror was excited by this act of sacrilege. Whatever his faults may have been, the murdered Archbishop had dared to stand up against the Crown for the rights of the Church, and had died rather than yield to the Kings demands. "For the name of Jesus and the defence of the Church I am ready to die," were his last words, as he fell under the assassins' blows. When he landed at Sandwich, on his return from France, the country folk crowded to meet him and hailed him as the father of orphans and deliverer of the oppressed, crying, "Blessed is he that cometh in the name of the Lord." His journey to Canterbury was one long triumphal procession. The poor looked to him as their champion and defender, who had laid down his life in the cause of freedom and righteousness. Henceforth Thomas became a national hero, and was everywhere honoured as the Martyr of the English.

The popular belief in his holiness was confirmed by the miracles that were wrought in his name from the moment of his death. A violent storm broke over the Cathedral when the fatal deed was done, and was followed by a red glow, which illuminated the choir where the dead man's body was laid before the altar. The next day the monks buried the corpse in a marble tomb behind Our Lady's altar in the under-croft. For nearly a year no mass was said in the Cathedral, no music was heard, no bells were rung; the altars were stripped of their ornaments, and the crucifixes and images were covered over. Meanwhile, reports reached Canterbury of the wonderful cures performed by the martyred Archbishop. On the third day after the murder, the wife of a Sussex knight, who suffered from blindness, invoked the blessed martyr's help, and was restored to sight. And on the very night of the burial the paralytic wife of a citizen of Canterbury was cured by a garment which her husband had dipped in the murdered saint's blood.

These marvels were followed by a stream of devout pilgrims who came to seek healing at the martyr's tomb or to pay their vows for the mercies which they had received. A monk was stationed at the grave to receive offerings and report the miracles that were wrought to the Chapter. At first these wonders were kept secret, for fear of the King, and of Becket's enemies, the De Brocs, whose men guarded the roads to Canterbury. The doors of the crypt were kept bolted and barred, and only the poor in the town and the neighbouring villages crept to the tomb. But on Easter Day, 1171, the crowds rushed in to see a dumb man who was said to have recovered his speech; and on the following Friday the crypt was thrown open to the public. From that time, writes Benedict, the monk of Canterbury, "the scene of the Pool of Bethesda was daily renewed in the Cathedral, and numbers of sick and helpless persons were to be seen lying on the pavement of the great church." "These great miracles are wrought," wrote John of Salisbury, an intimate friend of Becket, who became Bishop of Chartres in 1176, and was an able statesman and scholar, "in the place of his passion and in the place where he lay before the great altar before his burial, and in the tomb where he was laid at last, the blind see, the deaf hear, the dumb speak, the lame walk, lepers are cleansed, and, a thing unheard of since the days of our fathers, the dead are raised to life."

From all parts of England the sick and suffering now crowded to Canterbury, telling the same marvellous tale, how Thomas had appeared to them robed in white, with the thin red streak of blood across his face, bringing healing and peace. "In towns and villages, in castles and cottages, throughout the kingdom," writes another contemporary chronicler, "every one from the highest to the lowest wishes to visit and honour his tomb. Clerks and laymen, rich and poor, nobles and common people, fathers and mothers with their children, masters with their servants, all come hither, moved by the same spirit of devotion. They travel by day and night in winter and summer, however cold the weather may be, and the inns and hostelries on the road to Canterbury are as crowded with people as great cities are on market days."

On the 21st of February, 1173, Pope Alexander III. pronounced the decree of canonisation, and fixed the Feast of St. Thomas of Canterbury on the day of the Archbishop's martyrdom. In July, 1174, King Henry II., moved by the reports which reached him in Normandy of the popular enthusiasm for Becket, and fearing the effects of the divine wrath, came himself to do penance at the martyr's tomb. Three months after the King of the English had given this public proof of his penitence and obtained release from the Church's censures, "the glorious choir of Conrad" was destroyed by fire, on the night of September 5, 1174. The rebuilding of the church, which was largely assisted by offerings at Becket's tomb, was not finished until 1220, when the Saint's body was removed to its final resting-place in the new apse at the East end of the Chapel of the Blessed Trinity, where the Archbishop had said his first mass.

On Tuesday, July 7, an immense concourse of people of all ranks and ages assembled at Canterbury. "The city and villages round," writes an eye-witness, "were so filled with folk that many had to abide in tents or under the open sky." Free hospitality was given to all, and the streets of Canterbury literally flowed with wine. A stately procession, led by the young King Henry III. and the patriot Archbishop Stephen Langton, entered the crypt, and bore the Saint's remains with solemn ceremonial to their new resting-place. Here a sumptuous shrine, adorned with gold plates and precious gems, wrought "by the greatest master of the craft" that could be found in England, received the martyr's relics, and the new apse became known as "Becket's Crown."

The fame of St. Thomas now spread into all parts of the world during the next two centuries, and the Canterbury pilgrimage was the most popular in Christendom. The 7th of July was solemnly set apart as the Feast of the Translation of St. Thomas, and henceforth the splendour of this festival threw the anniversary of the actual martyrdom into the shade. The very fact that it took place in summer and not in winter naturally attracted greater numbers of pilgrims from a distance. And on the jubilees or fiftieth anniversaries of the Translation, the concourse of people assembled at Canterbury was enormous.

Besides the crowds attracted by these two chief festivals, pilgrims came to Canterbury in smaller parties at all seasons of the year, but more especially in the spring and summer months. Each year, as Chaucer sings, when the spring-time comes round,

"When that Aprille with his showers sweete
The drought of Marche had pierced to the roote....
When Zephyrus eke with his sweete breathe
Inspired hath in every holt and heathe
The tender croppes ...
And small fowlës maken melodie,
That sleepen all the night with open eye,
Then longen folk to go on pilgrimages,
And palmers for to seeken strange 'strandës' ...
And specially, from every shire's ende
Of Engelond, to Caunterbury they wende,
The holy blissful martyr for to seeke
That them hath holpen when that they were sicke."

The passage of these caravans of pilgrims could not fail to leave its mark on the places and the people along their path. The sight of these strange faces, the news they brought, and the tales they told must have impressed the dwellers in these quiet woodlands and lonely hills. And traces of their presence remain to this day on the Surrey downs and in the lanes of Kent. They may, or may not, have been responsible for the edible variety of large white snails, *Helix pomatia*, commonly called Roman snails, which are found in such abundance at Albury in Surrey, and at Charing in Kent, as well as at other places along the road, and which the Norman French pilgrims are traditionally said to have brought over with them. But the memory of their pilgrimage survives in the wayside chapels and shrines which sprung up along the track, in the churches which were built for their benefit, or restored and decorated by their devotion, above all in the local names still in common use along the countryside. Pilgrims' Lodge and Pilgrims' Ferry, Palmers' Wood, Paternoster Lane —these, and similar terms, still speak of the custom which had taken such fast hold of the popular mind during the three hundred and fifty years after the death of Becket, and recall the long processions of pilgrims which once wound over these lonely hills and through these green lanes on their way to the martyr's shrine.

CHAPTER II

WINCHESTER TO ALTON

Few traces of the Pilgrims' Way are now to be found in Hampshire. But early writers speak of an old road which led to Canterbury from Winchester, and the travellers' course would in all probability take them through this ancient city. Here the foreign pilgrims who landed at Southampton, and those who came from the West of England, would find friendly shelter in one or other of the religious houses, and enjoy a brief resting-time before they faced the perils of the road. The old capital of Wessex, the home of Alfred, and favourite residence of Saxon and Norman kings, had many attractions to offer to the devout pilgrim. Here was the splendid golden shrine of St. Swithun, the gentle Bishop who had watched over the boyhood of Alfred. In A.D. 971, a hundred years after the Saint's death, his bones had been solemnly removed from their resting-place on the north side of the Minster, where he had humbly begged to be buried" so that the sun might not shine upon him," and laid by Edgar and Dunstan behind the altar of the new Cathedral which Bishop Ethelwold had raised on the site of the ancient church of Birinus. This was done, says the chronicler Wulfstan, although the Saint himself "protested weeping that his body ought not to be set in God's holy church amidst the splendid memorials of the ancient fathers," a legend which may have given rise to the popular tradition of the forty days' rain, and the supposed delay in the Saint's funeral. From that time countless miracles were wrought at the shrine of St. Swithun, and multitudes from all parts of England flocked to seek blessing and healing at the great church which henceforth bore his name.

Under the rule of Norman and Angevin kings, the venerable city had attained the height of wealth and prosperity. In those days the population numbered some 20,000, and there are said to have been as many as 173 churches and chapels within its wall. In spite of the horrors of civil war, which twice desolated the streets, in the time of Stephen and Henry III., the frequent presence of the court and the energy of her prince-bishops had made Winchester a centre of religious and literary activity. And, although after the death of Henry III., who throughout his long life remained faithful to his native city, royal visits became few and far between, and the old capital lost something of its brilliancy, there was still much to attract strangers and strike the imagination of the wayfarer who entered her gates in the fifteenth century. Few mediæval cities could boast foundations of equal size and splendour. There was the strong castle of Wolvesey, where the bishops reigned in state, and the royal palace by the West gate, built by King Henry III., with the fair Gothic hall which he had decorated so lavishly. There was the Hospital of St. Cross, founded by the warrior-bishop, Henry de Blois, and the new College of St. Mary, which William of Wykeham, the great master-builder, had reared in the meadows known as the Greenery, or promenade of the monks of St. Swithun. Another venerable hospital, that of St. John's, claimed to have been founded by Birinus, and on Morne Hill, just outside the East gate, stood a hospital for lepers, dedicated to St. Mary Magdalene. There, conspicuous among a crowd of religious houses by their wealth and antiquity, were the two great Benedictine communities of St. Swithun and Hyde. And there, too, was the grand Norman church which the Conqueror's kinsman, Bishop Walkelin, had raised on the ruins of Ethelwold's Minster, with its low massive tower and noble transepts, and the long nave roofed in with solid trees of oak cut down in Hempage Wood. Three centuries later, William of Wykeham transformed the nave after the latest fashion of architecture, cut through the old Norman work, carried up the piers to a lofty height, and replaced the flat wooden roof by fine stone groining. But the Norman tower and transepts of Bishop Walkelin's church still remain to-day almost unchanged.

So great was the concourse of pilgrims to St. Swithun's shrine in the early part of the fourteenth century, that Bishop Godfrey Lucy enlarged the eastward portion of the church, and built, as it were, another church, with nave, aisles, and Lady Chapel of its own, under the same roof. The monks had no great love for the lower class of pilgrims who thronged their doors, and took good care to keep them out of the conventual precincts. They were only allowed to enter the Minster by a doorway in the north transept, and, once they had visited the shrine and duly made their offerings, they were jealously excluded from the rest of the church by those fine ironwork gates still preserved in the Cathedral, and said to be the oldest specimen of the kind in England.

Towards the close of the century, in the reign of Edward I., the fine old building still known as the Strangers' Hall was built by the monks of St. Swithun at their convent gate, for the reception of the poorer pilgrims. Here they found food and shelter for the night. They slept, ate their meals, and drank their ale, and made merry round one big central fire. The hall is now divided, and is partly used as the Dean's stable, partly enclosed in a Canon's house, but traces of rudely carved heads, a bearded king, and a nun's face are still visible on the massive timbers of the vaulted roof, blackened with the smoke of bygone ages. In the morning the same pilgrims would wend their way to the doors of the Prior's lodging, and standing under the three beautiful pointed arches which form the entrance to the present Deanery, would there receive alms in money and fragments of bread and meat to help them on their journey.

The route which they took on leaving Winchester is uncertain. It is not till we approach Alton that we find the first traces of the Pilgrims' Way, but in all probability they followed the Roman road which still leads to Silchester and London along the valley of the river Itchen. Immediately outside the city gates they would find themselves before another stately pile of conventual buildings, the great Abbey of Hyde. This famous Benedictine house, founded by Alfred, and long known as the New Minster, was first removed from its original site near the Cathedral in the twelfth century. Finding their house damp and unhealthy, and feeling themselves cramped in the narrow space close to the rival monastery of St. Swithun, the monks obtained a charter from Henry I. giving them leave to settle outside the North gate. In the year 1110, they moved to their new home, bearing with them the wonder-working shrine of St. Josse, the great silver cross given to the New Minster by Cnut, and a yet more precious relic, the bones of Alfred the Great. Here in the green meadows on the banks of the Itchen they reared the walls of their new convent and the magnificent church which, after being in the next reign burnt to the ground by fire-balls from Henry of Blois' Castle at Wolvesey, rose again from the flames fairer and richer than before. Here it stood till the Dissolution, when Thomas Wriothesley, Cromwell's Commissioner, stripped the shrine of its treasures, carried off the gold and jewels, and pulled down the abbey walls to use the stone in the building of his own great house at Stratton. "We intend," he wrote to his master, after describing the riches of gold and silver plate, the crosses studded with pearls, chalices, and emeralds on which he had lain sacrilegious hands, "both at Hyde and St. Mary to sweep away all the rotten bones that be called relics; which we may not omit, lest it be thought we came more for the treasure than for the avoiding of the abomination of idolatry." Considerable fragments of the building still remained. In Milner's time the ruins covered the whole meadow, but towards the end of the last century the city authorities fixed on the spot as the site of a new bridewell, and all that was left of the once famous Abbey was then destroyed. The tombs of the dead were rifled. At every stroke of the spade some ancient sepulchre was violated, stone coffins containing chalices, croziers, rings, were broken open and bones scattered abroad. Then the ashes of the noblest of our kings were blown to the winds, and the resting-place of Ælfred remains to this day unknown. A stone marked with the words, Ælfred Rex, DCCCLXXXI., was carried off by a passing stranger, and is now to be seen at Corby Castle, in Cumberland. To-day an old gateway near the church of St. Bartholomew and some fragments of the monastery wall are the only remains of Alfred's new Minster.

From this spot an ancient causeway, now commonly known as the Nuns' Walk, but which in the last century bore the more correct title of the Monks' Walk, leads alongside of a stream which supplied Hyde Abbey with water, for a mile and a half up the valley to Headbourne Worthy. The path is cool and shady, planted with a double row of tall elms, and as we look back we have beautiful views of the venerable city and the great Cathedral sleeping in the quiet hollow, dreaming of all its mighty past. Above, scarred with the marks of a deep railway cutting, and built over with new houses, is St. Giles' Hill, where during many centuries the famous fair was held each September. Foreign pilgrims would gaze with interest on the scene of that yearly event, which had attained a world-wide fame, and attracted merchants from all parts of France, Flanders, and Italy. The green hill-side from which we look down on the streets and towers of Winchester presented a lively spectacle during that fortnight. The stalls were arranged in long rows and called after the nationality of the vendors of the goods they sold. There was the Street of Caen, of Limoges, of the Flemings, of the Genoese, the Drapery, the Goldsmiths' Stall, the Spicery, held by the monks of St. Swithun, who drove a brisk trade in furs and groceries on these occasions. All shops in the city and for seven leagues round were closed during the fair, and local trade was entirely suspended. The mayor handed over the keys of the city for the time being to the bishop, who had large profits from the tolls and had stalls at the fair himself, while smaller portions went to the abbeys, and thirty marks a year were paid to St. Swithun's for the repair of the great church. The Red King first granted his kinsman, Bishop Walkelin, the tolls of this three days' fair at St. Giles' feast, which privilege was afterwards extended to a period of sixteen days by Henry III. The great fair lasted until modern times, but in due course was removed from St. Giles' Hill into the city itself. "As the city grew stronger and the fair weaker," writes Dean Kitchin, "it slid down St. Giles' Hill and entered the town, where its noisy ghost still holds revel once a year."

Leaving these historic memories behind us we follow the Monks' Walk until we reach Headbourne Worthy, the first of a group of villages granted by Egbert, in 825, to St. Swithun's Priory, and bearing this quaint name, derived from the Saxon *woerth*—a homestead. The church here dates from Saxon times, and claims to have been founded by St. Wilfred. The rude west doorway and chancel arch are said to belong to Edward the Confessor's time. Over the west archway, which now leads into a fifteenth-century chapel, is a fine sculptured bas-relief larger than life, representing the Crucifixion and the Maries, which probably originally adorned the exterior of the church. But the most interesting thing in the church is the brass to John Kent, a Winchester scholar, who died in 1434. The boy wears his college gown and his hair is closely cut, while a scroll comes out of his lips bearing the words: "Misericordiam Dni inetum cantabo." Next we reach Kingsworthy, so called because it was once Crown property, a pretty little village with low square ivy-grown church-tower and lych-gate, and a charming old-fashioned inn standing a little back from the road.

The third of the Worthys, Abbotsworthy, is now united to Kingsworthy. Passing through its little street of houses, a mile farther on we reach Martyrsworthy, a still smaller village with another old Norman church and low thatched cottages, picturesquely placed near the banks of the river, which is here crossed by a wooden foot-bridge. But all this part of the Itchen valley has the same charm. Everywhere we find the same old farmhouses with mullioned windows and sundials and yew trees, the same straggling roofs brilliant with yellow lichen, and the same cottages and gardens gay with lilies and phloxes, the same green lanes shaded with tall elms and poplars, the same low chalk hills and wooded distances closing in the valley, and below the bright river winding its way through the cool meadows. "The Itchen—the beautiful Itchen valley," exclaims Cobbett, as he rides along this vale of meadows. "There are few spots in England more fertile, or more pleasant, none, I believe, more healthy. The fertility of this vale and of the surrounding country is best proved by the fact that, besides the town of Alresford and that of Southampton, there are seventeen villages, each having its parish church, upon its borders. When we consider these things, we are not surprised that a spot situated about half-way down this vale should have been chosen for the building of a city, or that that city should have been for a great number of years the place of residence for the kings of England."

Towards Itchen Abbas—of the Abbot—the valley opens, and we see the noble avenues and spreading beeches of Avington Park, long the property of the Dukes of Chandos, and often visited by Charles II. while Wren was building his red-brick palace at Winchester. Here the Merry Monarch feasted his friends in a banqueting-hall that is now a greenhouse, and a room in the old house bore the name of Nell Gwynne's closet. In those days it was the residence of the notorious Lady Shrewsbury, afterwards the wife of George Brydges, a member of the Chandos family, the lady whose first husband, Francis, Earl of Shrewsbury, was slain fighting in a duel with George Villiers, Duke of

Buckingham, while the Countess herself, disguised as a page, held her lover's horse.

The river winds through the park, and between the over-arching boughs of the forest trees we catch lovely glimpses of wood and water. In the opposite direction, but also close to Itchen Abbas, is another well-known seat, Lord Ashburton's famous Grange, often visited by Carlyle. Here the dark tints of yew and fir mingle with the bright hues of lime and beech and silver birch on the banks of a clear lake, and long grassy glades lead up to wild gorse-grown slopes of open down. Still following the river banks we reach Itchen Stoke, another picturesque village with timbered cottages and mossy roofs. A little modern church, with high-pitched roof and lancet windows having a curiously foreign air, stands among the tall pines on a steep bank above the stream. But here our pleasant journey along the fair Itchen valley comes to an end, and, leaving the river-side, we climb the hilly road which leads us into Alresford.

New Alresford, a clean, bright little town, with broad street, planted with rows of trees, boasts an antiquity which belies its name, and has been a market-town and borough from time immemorial. Like its yet more venerable neighbour, Old Alresford, it was given by a king of the West Saxons to the prior and monks of St. Swithun at Winchester, and formed part of the vast possessions of the monastery at the Conquest. Both places took their name from their situation on a ford of the Arle or Alre river, a considerable stream which joins the Itchen below Avington, and is called by Leland the Alresford river. In the eleventh century New Alresford had fallen into decay, and probably owes its present existence to Bishop Godfrey Lucy, who rebuilt the town, and obtained a charter from King John restoring the market, which had fallen into disuse. At the same time he gave the town the name of New Market, but the older one survived, and the Bishop's new title was never generally adopted. The same energetic prelate bestowed a great deal of care and considerable attention on the water supply of Winchester, and made the Itchen navigable all the way from Southampton to Alresford.

In recognition of this important service, Bishop Lucy received from King John the right of levying toll on all leather, hides, and other goods which entered Winchester by the river Itchen through this canal, a right which descended to his successors in the see. South-west of the town is the large pond or reservoir which he made to supply the waters of the Itchen. This lake, which still covers about sixty acres, is a well-known haunt of moor-hens and other waterfowl, and the flags and bulrushes which fringe its banks make it a favourable resort of artists. Old Alresford itself, with its gay flower-gardens, tall elms, pretty old thatched cottages grouped round the village green, may well supply them with more than one subject for pen and pencil.

New Alresford was at one time a flourishing centre of the cloth trade, in which the Winchester merchants drove so brisk a trade at St. Giles' Fair. The manufacture of woollen cloth was carried on till quite recent times, and Dean Kitchin tells us that there are old men still living who remember driving with their fathers to the fair at Winchester on St. Giles' day, to buy a roll of blue cloth to provide the family suits for the year. But New Alresford shared the decline as it had shared the prosperity of its more important neighbour, and suffered even more severely than Winchester in the Civil Wars, when the town was almost entirely burnt down by Lord Hopton's troops after their defeat in Cheriton fight. The scene of that hard-fought battle, which gave Winchester into Waller's hands and ruined the King's cause in the West of England, lies a few miles to the south of Alresford. Half-way between the two is Tichborne Park, the seat of a family which has owned this estate from the days of Harold, and which took its name from the stream flowing through the parish, and called the Ticceborne in Anglo-Saxon records. In modern times a well-known case has given the name of Tichborne an unenviable notoriety, but members of this ancient house have been illustrious at all periods of our history, and the legend of the Tichborne Dole so long associated with the spot deserves to be remembered. In the reign of Henry I., Isabella, the wife of Sir Roger Tichborne, a lady whose long life had been spent in deeds of mercy, prayed her husband as she lay dying to grant her as much land as would enable her to leave a dole of bread for all who asked alms at the gates of Tichborne on each succeeding Lady Day. Sir Roger was a knight of sterner stuff, and seizing a flaming brand from the hearth he told his wife jestingly that she might have as much land as she could herself walk over before the burning torch went out. Upon which the sick lady caused herself to be borne from her bed to a piece of ground within the manor, and crawled on her knees and hands until she had encircled twenty-three acres. The actual plot of ground still bears the name of Lady Tichborne's Crawles, and there was an old prophecy which said that the house of Tichborne would only last as long as the dying bequest of Isabella was carried out. During the next six centuries, nineteen hundred small loaves were regularly distributed to the poor at the gates on Lady Day, and a miraculous virtue was supposed to belong to bread thus bestowed. The custom was only abandoned a hundred years ago, owing to the number of idlers and bad characters which it brought into the neighbourhood, and a sum of money equal in amount to the Dole is given to the poor of the parish in its stead.

Whether any of our Canterbury pilgrims stopped in their course to avail themselves of the Tichborne Dole we cannot say, but there was a manor-house of the Bishops of Winchester at Bishop Sutton, near Alresford, where they would no doubt find food and shelter. Nothing now remains of the episcopal palace, and no trace of its precincts is preserved but the site of the bishop's kennels.

After crossing the river at Alresford the pilgrims turned north-east, and according to an old tradition their road led them through the parish of Ropley, a neighbouring village where Roman remains have been discovered. A little further on the same track, close to Rotherfield Park, where the modern mansion of Pelham now stands, was an ancient house which bore the name of Pilgrims' Place, and is indicated as such in old maps.

CHAPTER III

ALTON TO COMPTON

A FEW miles to the right of the road is a place which no pilgrim of modern times can leave unvisited—Selborne, White's Selborne, the home of the gentle naturalist whose memory haunts these rural scenes. Here he lived in the picturesque house overgrown with creepers, with the sunny garden and dial at the back, and the great spreading oak where he loved to study the ways of the owls, and the juniper tree, which, to his joy, survived the Siberian winter of 1776. And here he died, and lies buried in the quiet churchyard in the shade of the old yew tree where he so often stood to watch his favourite birds. Not a stone but what speaks of him, not a turn in the village street but has its tale to tell. The playstow, or village green, which Adam de Gurdon granted to the Augustinian Canons of Selborne in the thirteenth century, where the prior held his market of old, and where young and old met on summer evenings under the big oak, and "sat in quiet debate" or "frolicked and danced" before him; the farmhouse which now marks the site of the ancient Priory itself, founded by Peter de Rupibus, Bishop of Winchester, in 1232—he has described them all. How the good Canons grew lazy and secular in their ways after a time, how William of Wykeham found certain of them professed hunters and sportsmen, and tried in vain to reform them, and how the estates were finally handed over to the new college of St. Mary Magdalene at Oxford, by its founder, William of Waynflete—Gilbert White has already told us. The Hanger, with its wooded slopes, rising from the back of his garden, and that "noble chalk promontory" of Nore Hill, planted with the beeches which he called the most lovely of all forest trees, how familiar they seem to us! Still the swifts wheel to and fro round the low church-tower, and the crickets chirp in the long grass, and the white owl is heard at night, just as when he used to linger under the old walls and watch their manners with infinite care and love.

One of the "rocky hollow lanes" which lead towards Alton will take us back into the road, and bring us to Chawton, a village about a mile from that town. The fine Elizabethan manor-house at the foot of the green knoll, and the grey church peeping out of the trees close by, have been for centuries the home and burial-place of the Knights. On the south side of the chancel a black and white marble monument records the memory of that gallant cavalier, Sir Richard Knight, who risked life and fortune in the Royal cause, and was invested with the Order of the Royal Oak by Charles II. after the Restoration. But it is as the place where Jane Austen, in George Eliot's opinion, "the greatest artist that has ever written," composed her novels, that Chawton is memorable. The cottage where she lived is still standing a few hundred yards from the "great house," which was the home of the brother and nieces to whom she was so fondly attached. She and her sister, Cassandra, settled there in 1809, and remained there until May, 1817, when they moved to the corner house of College Street, Winchester, where three months afterwards she died. During the eight years spent in this quiet home, Jane Austen attained the height of her powers and wrote her most famous novels, those works which she herself said cost her so little, and which in Tennyson's words have given her a place in English literature "next to Shakespeare." "Sense and Sensibility," her first novel, was published two years after the move to Chawton. "Persuasion," the last and most finished of the immortal series, was only written in 1816, a year before her death. Seldom, indeed, has so great a novelist led so retired an existence. The life at Chawton, so smooth in its even flow, with the daily round of small excitements and quiet pleasures, the visits to the "great house," and walks with her nieces in the woods, the shopping expeditions to Alton, the talk about new bonnets and gowns, and the latest news as to the births, deaths, and marriages of the numerous relatives in Kent and Hampshire, are faithfully reflected in those pleasant letters of Jane Austen, which her great-nephew, Lord Brabourne, gave to the world. There is a good deal about her flowers, her chickens, her niece's love affairs, the fancy work on which she is engaged, the improvements in the house and garden—"You cannot imagine," she writes on one occasion, "it is not in human nature to imagine, what a nice walk we have round the orchard!"—but very little indeed about her books. Almost the only allusion we find to one of her characters is in 1816, when she writes to Fanny Knight of Anne Elliot in "Persuasion." "*You* may perhaps like the heroine, as she is almost too good for me!" Anything like fame or publicity was positively distasteful to her. She owns to feeling absolutely terrified when a lady in town asked to be introduced to her, and then adds laughingly, "If I am a wild beast I cannot help it, it is not my fault!"

Curiously enough, the Pilgrims' Way, in the later course of its path, brings us to Godmersham, that other and finer home of the Knights on the Kentish Downs, a place also associated with Jane Austen's life and letters, where she spent many pleasant hours in the midst of her family, enjoying the beauty of the spot and its cheerful surroundings. But Chawton retains the supremacy as her own home, and as the scene of those literary labours that were cut short, alas! too soon. "What a pity," Sir Walter Scott exclaimed, after reading a book of hers, "what a pity such a gifted creature died so early!"

From Chawton it is a short mile to Alton, famous for its breweries and hop gardens, and its church door, riddled with the bullets of the Roundheads. Our way now leads us through the woods of Alice Holt—Aisholt—the Ash wood; like Woolmer, a royal forest from Saxon times. Alice Holt was renowned for the abundance of its fallow deer, which made it a favourite hunting ground with the Plantagenet kings, and on one occasion Edward II., it is said, gave one of his scullions, Morris Ken, the sum of twenty shillings because he fell from his horse so often out hunting, "which made the king laugh exceedingly." Here, too, after the battle of Evesham, Edward, Prince of Wales, defeated Adam de Gurdon, one of Simon de Montfort's chief followers. He is said to have challenged the rebel baron to a single combat, in which Gurdon was wounded and made prisoner, but the victor spared his life and afterwards obtained a royal pardon for his vanquished foe. A wild rugged tract of country, Alice Holt was a chosen haunt of robbers and outlaws, the terror of the wealthy London merchants who journeyed to St. Giles' Fair at Winchester, and in the fourteenth century the wardens of the fair kept five mounted serjeants-at-arms in the forest near Alton, for their protection at that season.

Soon after leaving Alton the pilgrims would catch their first sight of the river Wey, which rises close to the town. Along the banks of this stream, flowing as it does through some of the loveliest Surrey scenery, their road was now to lie, and not until they crossed St. Katherine's ferry, at Guildford, were they finally to lose sight of its waters. The river itself, more than one writer has suggested, may owe its name to this circumstance, and have been originally called the Way river from the ancient road which followed the early part of its course.

Leaving Froyle Park, Sir Hubert Miller's fine Jacobean house, on our left, we pass Bentley Station, and, still following the river, join the Portsmouth road just before entering Farnham. This town, which takes its name from the commons overgrown with fern and heather still to be seen in the neighbourhood on the Surrey side, is now surrounded with hop gardens. It was among the earliest possessions of the Bishops of Winchester, and formed part of the land granted to St. Swithun, in 860, by Alfred's elder brother, Ethelbald, King of Wessex. The Castle-palace, which still looks proudly down on the streets of the little town, was first built by that magnificent prelate, Henry of Blois, but little of the original building now remains except the offices, where some round Norman pillars may still be seen. Farnham Castle was partly destroyed by Henry III. during his wars with the barons, and suffered greatly at the hands of the rebels in the time of Charles I., but was afterwards rebuilt by Bishop Morley. Queen Elizabeth paid frequent visits here, and on one occasion, while dining in the great hall with the Duke of Norfolk, who was suspected of planning a marriage with Mary Queen of Scots, pleasantly advised the Duke to be careful on what pillow he laid his head. The lawn, with its stately cedars and grass-grown moat, deserves a visit, but the most interesting part of the building is the fine old keep with its massive buttresses and thirteenth-century arches, commanding a wide view over the elm avenues of the park, and the commons which stretch eastward on the Surrey side. Prominent in the foreground are the picturesque heights of Crooksbury, crowned with those tall pines which Cobbett climbed when he was a boy, to take the nests of crows and magpies.

Farnham, it must be remembered, was the birthplace of this remarkable man, and it was at Ash, a small town at the foot of the Hog's Back, that he died in 1835. All his life long he retained the fondest affection for these scenes of his youth. In 1825 he brought his son Richard, then a boy of eleven, to see the little old house in the street where he had lived with his grandmother, and showed him the garden at Waverley where he worked as a lad, the tree near the Abbey from which he fell into the river in a perilous attempt to take a crow's nest, and the strawberry beds where he gathered strawberries for Sir Robert Rich's table, taking care to eat the finest! Among these hills and commons, where he followed the hounds on foot at ten years old, and rode across country at seventy, we forget the political aspect of his life, his bitter invectives against the Poor-laws and Paper-money, the National Debt and the System, and think rather of his keen love of nature and delight in the heaths, the sandy coppices, and forests of Surrey and Hampshire. And now he sleeps in the church of Farnham, where he desired to be buried, in the heart of the wild scenery which he loved so well.

Just under Crooksbury, that "grand scene" of Cobbett's "exploits," lies Moor Park, the retreat of Sir William Temple in his old age, which seemed to him, to quote his own words, "the sweetest place, I think, that I have ever seen in my life, either before or since, at home or abroad." There we may still see the gardens which the statesman of the Triple Alliance laid out after the fashion of those which he remembered in Holland, where he enjoyed the companionship of his beloved sister, Lady Giffard, and where his heart lies buried under the sundial. Here Swift lived as his secretary, and learnt from King William III. how to cut asparagus; here he wrote the "Tale of a Tub," and made love to Mrs. Hester Johnson, Lady Giffard's pretty black-eyed waiting-maid. The memory of that immortal love-story has not yet perished, and the house where she lived is still known as Stella's Cottage. Here, too, just beyond Moor Park, on the banks of the Wey, are the ruins of Waverley Abbey, the first Cistercian house ever founded in England, often described as "le petit Cîteaux," and the mother of many other abbeys.

The more distinguished pilgrims who stopped at Farnham would taste the hospitality of the monks of Waverley, and Henry III. was on one occasion their guest. The Abbot of Waverley, too, was a great personage in these parts, and his influence extended over several parishes through which the pilgrims had to pass, although the privileges which he claimed were often disputed by the Prior of Newark, the other ecclesiastical magnate who reigned in this part of Surrey. Pilgrims of humbler rank would find ample accommodation in the ancient hostelries of Farnham, which was at that time a place of considerable importance, and returned two members to Edward II.'s Parliament.

Their onward course now lay along the banks of the Wey until they reached the foot of the narrow, curiously shaped chalk ridge known as the Hog's Back. Here, at a place called Whiteway End, the end of the white chalk road, two roads divide. Both lead to Guildford, the one keeping on the crest of the ridge, the other along its southern slope.

The upper road has become an important thoroughfare in modern times, and is now the main road from Farnham to Guildford; the lower is a grassy lane, not always easy to follow, and little used in places, which leads through the parishes of Seale, Puttenham, and Compton, the bright little villages which stud the sides of the Hog's Back. This green woodland path under the downs was the ancient British and Roman track along which the Canterbury pilgrims journeyed, and which is still in some places spoken of by the inhabitants as the Way. Other names in local use bear the same witness. Beggar's Corner and Robber's or Roamer's Moor are supposed to owe their appellations to the pilgrims: while the ivy-grown manor-house of Shoelands, bearing the date of 1616 on its porch, is said to take its name from the word "to shool," which in some dialects has the same meaning as "to beg."

Another trace of the Pilgrimage is to be found in the local fairs which are still held in the towns and villages along the road, and which were fixed at those periods of the year when the pilgrims would be either going to Canterbury or returning from there. Thus we find that at Guildford the chief fair took place at Christmas, when the pilgrims would be on their way to the winter festival of St. Thomas, and was only altered to September in 1312, by which time the original day of the Saint's martyrdom had ceased to be as popular as the summer feast. Again the great fair at Shalford was fixed for the Feast of the Assumption, the 15th of August, so as to catch the stream of pilgrims which flowed back from Canterbury after the Feast of the Translation in July, and the seven days' fair there, that went by the name of Becket's fair. Fairs soon came to be held not only at towns such as Farnham, Guildford, and Shalford, but at the small villages along the Pilgrims' Road. There was one in the churchyard at Puttenham, and another at Wanborough, a church on the northern side of the hill, which belonged to Waverley Abbey, where the offerings made by the pilgrims formed part of the payments yearly received by the Abbot, while a third was held on St. Katharine's Hill during five days in September.

Even the churches along the road often owed their existence to the Pilgrimage. The church of Seale was built early in the thirteenth century by the Abbots of Waverley, and that of Wanborough was rebuilt by the same Abbots, and was again allowed to fall into decay when the days of pilgrimages were over. Both the sister chapels of St. Katharine and St. Martha, we shall see, owed their restoration to the pilgrims' passage, and many more along the Way were either raised in honour of St. Thomas, or else adorned with frescoes and altar-pieces of the Martyrdom.

Along this pleasant Surrey hill-side the old Canterbury pilgrims journeyed, going from church to church, from shrine to shrine, and more especially if their pilgrimage took place in summer, enjoying the sweet country air and leafy shades of this quiet woodland region. They lingered, we may well believe, at the village fairs, and stopped at every town to see the sights and hear the news; for the pilgrim of mediæval days was, as Dean Stanley reminds us, a traveller with the same adventures, stories, pleasures, pains, as the traveller of our own times, and men of every type and class set out on pilgrimages much as tourists to-day start on a foreign trip. Some, no doubt, undertook the journey from devotion, and more in a vague hope of reaping some profit, both material and spiritual, from a visit to the shrine of the all-powerful Saint, while a thousand other motives—curiosity, love of change and adventure, the pleasure of a journey—prompted the crowds who thronged the road at certain seasons of the year. Chaucer's company of pilgrims we know was a motley crew, and included men and women whose characters were as varied as their rank and trade. With them came a throng of jugglers and story-tellers and minstrels, who beguiled the way with music and laughter as they rode or walked along, so that "every town they came through, what with the noise of their singing, and with the sound of their piping, and with the jangling of their Canterbury bells, and with the barking of the dogs after them, they made more noise than if the king came there with all his clarions." In their train, too, a crowd of idle folk, of roving pedlars and begging friars and lazy tramps, who were glad of any excuse to beg a crust or coin.

The presence of these last was by no means always welcome at the inns and religious houses on the road, where doubtful characters often craved admittance, knowing that if the hand of justice overtook them they could always find refuge in one of those churches where the rights of sanctuary were so resolutely claimed and so jealously defended by the Abbot of Waverley or the Prior of Newark.

CHAPTER IV

COMPTON TO SHALFORD

FOLLOWING the Pilgrims' Way along the southern slopes of the Hog's Back, we cross Puttenham Heath, and reach the pretty little village of Compton. Here, nestling under the downs, a few hundred yards from the track, is a beautiful old twelfth-century church, which was there before the days of St. Thomas. This ancient structure, dedicated to St. Nicholas, still retains some good stained glass and boasts a unique feature in the shape of a double-storied chancel. The east end of the church is crossed by a low semicircular arch enriched with Norman zigzag moulding, and surmounted by a rude screen, which is said to be the oldest piece of wood-work in England. Both the upper and the lower sanctuaries have piscinas, and there is an Early English one in the south aisle. The massive bases of the chalk pillars, the altar-tomb north of the chancel— probably an Eastern sepulchre—and a hagioscope now blocked up, all deserve attention, as well as the fine Jacobean pulpit and chancel screen, which is now placed under the tower arch.

A mile to the west of this singularly interesting church is Loseley, the historic mansion of the More and Molyneux family. This manor was Crown property in the reign of Edward the Confessor, and is described in Domesday Book as the property of the Norman Roger de Montgomery, Earl of Shrewsbury, on whom it was bestowed by the Conqueror. After passing through many hands it was finally bought from the Earl of Gloucester, early in the sixteenth century, by Sir Christopher More, whose son, Sir William, built the present mansion. The grand old house with its grey-stone gables and mullioned windows is a perfect specimen of Elizabethan architecture. The broad grass terrace along the edge of the moat, the yew hedges with their glossy hues of green and purple, the old-fashioned borders full of bright flowers, and the low pigeon-houses standing at each angle, all remain as they were in the reign of James I., and agree well with Lord Bacon's idea of what a pleasance ought to be. Within, the walls are wainscoted with oak panelling throughout, and the ceilings and mantelpieces are richly decorated. The cross and mulberry tree of the Mores, with their mottoes, may still be seen in the stained-glass oriel of the great hall, and on the cornices of the drawing-room. Here too is a fine mantelpiece, carved in white chalk, which is said to have been designed by Hans Holbein. Many are the royal visitors who have left memorials of their presence at Loseley. Queen Elizabeth had an especial affection for the place, and was here three times. The cushioned seats of two gilt chairs were worked by her needle, and there is a painted panel bearing the quaint device of a flower-pot with the red and white roses of York and Lancaster, and the fleur-de-lis, with the words *Rosa Electa* and *Felicior Phœnice*, a pretty conceit which would not fail to find favour in the eyes of the Virgin Queen. The hall contains portraits of James I. and his wife Anne of Denmark, painted by Mytens in honour of a visit which they paid to Loseley in the first year of this monarch's reign; and the ceiling of his Majesty's bedroom is elaborately patterned over with stucco reliefs of Tudor roses and lilies and thistles. A likeness of Anne Boleyn, and several fine portraits of members of the More family, also adorn the walls, and there is a beautiful little picture of the boy-king, Edward VI., wearing an embroidered crimson doublet and jewelled cap and feather, painted by some clever pupil of Holbein in 1547. This portrait was sent in 1890 to the Tudor Exhibition, which also contained many historical documents relating to different personages of this royal line, preserved among the Loseley manuscripts. There are warrants signed by Edward VI., the Lord Protector, by Queen Elizabeth and the Lord of her Council, including Hatton the Lord Chancellor, Cecil, Lord Burghley, Lord Effingham, and Lord Derby. There is one of 1540, signed by Henry VIII., commanding Christopher More, Sheriff of the County of Sussex, to deliver certain goods forfeited to the crown to "Katheryn Howarde, one of our quene's maidens," and another, signed by Elizabeth in the first year of her reign, commanding William More to raise and equip one hundred able men, for the defence of England against foreign invasion. There is also a curious sumptuary proclamation by

Queen Elizabeth respecting the dress and ornaments of women, and, what is still more rare and interesting, a warrant from Lady Jane Grey, dated July 19, I. Jane, and signed "Jane the Quene." Among the more private and personal papers is an amusing letter from Robert Horne, Bishop of Winchester, giving Mr. More, of Loseley, advice as to stocking the new pond with the best kind of carp, "thes be of a little heade, broade side and not long; soche as be great headed and longe, made after the fashion of an herring, are not good, neither will ever be." Another from Bishop Day informs Sir William More, in 1596, that he intends to fish the little pond at Frensham; while one to the same gentleman from Alexander Nowell, Dean of St. Paul's, thanks him for his exertions to recover a stolen nag on his behalf. The treasures of Loseley, in fact, are as inexhaustible as its beauty.

A pleasant walk through the forest trees and grassy glades of the park leads us back to Compton village and the green lanes through which the Pilgrims' Way now wanders. Skirting the grounds of Monk's Hatch, with their pine-groves and rose-gardens lying under the chalk hanger, the old road passes close to Limnerslease, the Surrey home of George Frederic Watts. To-day thousands of pilgrims from all parts of the world seek out this sylvan retreat where the great master spent his last years, and visit the treasures of art which adorn its galleries, and the fair chapel and cloister that mark the painter's grave.

From Compton a path known as "Sandy Lane" leads over the hill past Brabœuf Manor, and the site of the old roadside shrine of Littleton Cross, and comes out on the open down, close to the chapel of St. Katherine. This now ruined shrine, which stands on a steep bank near the road, was rebuilt on the site of a still older one in 1317, by Richard de Wauncey, Rector of St. Nicholas, Guildford, and was much frequented by pilgrims to Canterbury. So valuable were the revenues derived by the parson from their offerings that the original grant made to Richard de Wauncey was disputed, and for some years the Rector of St. Mary stepped into his rights. But in 1329 the Rector of St. Nicholas succeeded in ousting his rival, and the chapel was re-consecrated and attached to the parish of St. Nicholas. An old legend ascribes the building of this shrine and of the chapel on St. Martha's Hill to two giant sisters of primæval days, who raised the walls with their own hands and flung their enormous hammer backwards and forwards from one hill to the other. Unlike its more fortunate sister-shrine, St. Katherine's chapel has long been roofless and dismantled, but it still forms a very picturesque object in the landscape, and the pointed arches of its broken windows frame in lovely views of the green meadows of the winding Wey, with the castle and churches of Guildford at our feet, and the hills and commons stretching far away, to the blue ridge of Hindhead.

The ancient city of Guildford owes its name and much of its historic renown to its situation on the chief ford of the river Wey, which here makes a break in the ridge of chalk downs running across Surrey. Guildford is mentioned in his will by King Alfred, who left it to his nephew Ethelwold, and became memorable as the spot where another Alfred, the son of Knut and Emma, was treacherously seized and murdered by Earl Godwin, who, standing on the eastern slope of the Hog's Back above the city, bade the young prince look back and see how large a kingdom would be his. For seven centuries, from the days of the Saxon kings to those of the Stuarts, Guildford remained Crown property, and the Norman keep which still towers grandly above the city was long a royal palace. The strength of the castle and importance of the position made it famous in the wars of the barons, and the Waverley annalist records its surrender to Louis VIII. of France, when he marched against King John from Sandwich Haven to Winchester. To-day the picturesqueness of the streets, the gabled roofs and panelled houses, and even more the situation of the town in the heart of this fair district, attract many artists, and make it a favourite centre for tourists.

In mediæval times Guildford was a convenient halting-place for pilgrims on their way from the south and west of England to the shrine of St. Thomas. Many of these, however, as the shrewd parson of St. Nicholas saw, when he thought it worth his while to buy the freehold of the site on which St. Katherine's chapel stood, would push on and cross the river by the ferry at the foot of the hill, which still bears the name of the Pilgrims' Ferry. On landing they found themselves in the parish of Shalford, in the meadows where the great fair was held each year in August. When the original charter was granted by King John, the fair took place in the churchyard, but soon the concourse of people became so great that it spread into the fields along the river, and covered as much as one hundred and forty acres of ground. Shalford Fair seems, in fact, to have been the most important one in this part of Surrey, and no doubt owed its existence to the passage of the Canterbury pilgrims.

CHAPTER V

SHALFORD TO ALBURY

THE line of the Pilgrims' Way may be clearly followed from the banks of the Wey up the hill. It goes through Shalford Park, up Ciderhouse Lane, where the ancient Pesthouse or refuge for sick pilgrims and travellers, now called Ciderhouse Cottage, is still standing, and leads through the Chantrey Woods straight to St. Martha's Chapel.

The district through which it takes us is one of the wildest and loveliest parts of Surrey. "Very few prettier rides in England," remarks Cobbett, who repeatedly travelled along this track, and the beauty of the views all along its course will more than repay the traveller who makes his way on foot over the hills from Guildford to Dorking. One of the most extensive is to be had from St. Martha's Hill, where the prospect ranges in one direction over South Leith Hill and the South Downs far away to the Weald of Sussex and the well-known clump of Chanctonbury Ring; and on the other over the commons and moors to the crests of Hindhead and the Hog's Back; while looking northward we have a wide view over the Surrey plains and the valley of the Thames, and Windsor Castle and the dome of St. Paul's may be distinguished on clear days.

The ancient chapel on the summit, which gives its name to St. Martha's Hill, was originally built in memory of certain Christians who suffered martyrdom on the spot, and was formerly dedicated to all holy martyrs, while the hill itself was known as the Martyrs' Hill, of which, as Grose remarks, "the present name is supposed to be a corruption." In the twelfth century it became peculiarly associated with the Canterbury pilgrims, and a new chancel was built for their use, and consecrated to St. Thomas à Becket in the year 1186. In 1262 this chapel was attached to the Priory of Newark, an Augustinian convent near Ripley, dedicated to St. Thomas of Canterbury by Ruald de Calva in the reign of Richard Cœur de Lion. The Prior already owned most of the hill-side, and the names of Farthing Copse and Halfpenny Lane, through which the pilgrims passed on their way to St. Martha's Chapel, remind us of the tolls which he levied from all who travelled along the road. We have already seen how in the earlier portions of the Way the Prior of Newark disputed the rights of the Abbot of Waverley. Here he reigned supreme. A priest from Newark Priory served St. Martha's Chapel, and is said to have lived at Tyting's Farm, an old gabled house with the remains of a small oratory close to the Pilgrims' Way. In latter days a colony of monks from Newark settled at Chilworth, where the present manor-house contains fragments of monastic building, and the fishponds of the friars may still be seen near the terraced gardens. During the troubled times of the Wars of the Roses the Chapel of St. Martha fell into ruins, and owed its restoration to Bishop William of Waynflete, who in 1463 granted forty days' indulgence to all pilgrims who should visit the shrine and there repeat a Pater Noster, an Ave, and a Credo, or contribute to its repair. After the dissolution of the monasteries both Newark Priory and St. Martha's shrine fell into ruins, and the chapel was only restored of late years. At Chilworth, south of St. Martha's Hill, lies the once fair valley which has been defaced by the powder-mills, first established there three centuries ago by an ancestor of John Evelyn, and now worked by steam. This is the place which Cobbett denounces in his "Rural Rides" with a vigour and eloquence worthy of Mr. Ruskin himself:

"This valley, which seems to have been created by a bountiful Providence as one of the choicest retreats of man, which seems formed for a scene of innocence and happiness, has been by ungrateful man so perverted as to make it instrumental in effecting two of the most damnable of purposes, in carrying into execution two of the most damnable inventions that ever sprang from the mind of man under the influence of the devil! namely, the making of gunpowder and of bank-notes! Here, in this tranquil spot, where the nightingales are to be heard earlier and later in the year than in any other part of England; where the first budding of the buds is seen in spring; where no rigour of season can ever be felt; where everything seems formed for precluding the very thought of wickedness; here has the devil fixed on as one of the seats of this grand manufactory; and perverse and ungrateful man not only lends his aid, but lends it cheerfully. To think that the springs which God has commanded to flow from the sides of these happy hills for the comfort and delight of man—to think that these springs should be perverted into means of spreading misery over a whole nation!"

One of these "inventions of the devil" has been removed. The paper-mills which made the bank-notes in Cobbett's time are silent now, but the powder-mills are in full activity, and Chilworth, with its coal-stores and railway-crossing, has a blackened and desolate look which not all the natural beauties of its surroundings can dispel.

Once more upon the hills, we can follow the line of yews which are seen at intervals along the ridge from St. Martha's Chapel by Weston Wood and the back of Albury Park, turning a few steps out of our path to visit Newland's Corner, the highest point of Albury Downs, and one of the most beautiful spots in the whole of Surrey. The view is as extensive as that from St. Martha's Hill, and is even more varied and picturesque. Over broken ridges of heathery down and gently swelling slopes, clad with beech and oak woods, we look across to Ewhurst Mill, a conspicuous landmark in all this country, and farther westward to the towers of Charterhouse and the distant heights of Hindhead and Blackdown; while immediately in front, across the wooded valley, rises St. Martha's Hill, crowned by its ancient chapel. Here we can watch the changes of sun and shower over the wide expanse of level country, and see the long range of far hills veiled in the thin blue mists of morning, or turning purple under the gold of the evening sky. Some of the oldest and finest yew trees in all Surrey are close to Newland's Corner—the ancient yew grove there is mentioned in Domesday—and their dark foliage offers a fine contrast to the bright tints of the neighbouring woods and to the snowy masses of blossom which in early summer clothe the gnarled old hawthorn trees that are studded over the hill-side. We can follow the track over the springy turf of the open downs and up glades thick with bracken, till it becomes choked with bushes and brambles, and finally loses itself in the woods of Albury.

Here, in the middle of the Duke of Northumberland's park, is the deep glen, surrounded by wooded heights, known as the Silent Pool. A dark tale, which Martin Tupper has made the subject of his "Stephen Langton," belongs to this lonely spot. King John, tradition says, loved a fair woodman's daughter who lived here, and surprised her in the act of bathing in the pool. The frightened girl let loose the branch by which she held, and was drowned in the water; and her brother, a goat-herd, who at the sound of her scream had rushed in after her, shared the same fate. And still, the legend goes, at midnight you may see a black-haired maiden clasping her arms round her brother in his cowhide tunic under the clear rippling surface of the Silent Pool.

A little farther on is the old church of Albury—Eldeburie, mentioned in Domesday, and supposed to be the most ancient in Surrey. The low tower, with its narrow two-light windows, probably dates back to very early Norman times, but the rest of the church is considerably later. The south chapel was richly decorated by Mr. Drummond, who bought the place in 1819, and is now used as a mortuary chapel for his family. Albury formerly belonged to the Dukes of Norfolk. The gardens were originally laid out by Thomas Howard, Earl of Arundel, the accomplished collector of the Arundel marbles, and whose fine portrait by Vandyck was exhibited at Burlington House in the winter of 1891. His friend and neighbour, Mr. Evelyn, helped him with his advice and taste, and designed the grotto under the hill, which still remains. "Such a Pausilippe," remarks the author of "The Sylva," "is nowhere in England besides." But the great ornament of Albury is the famous yew hedge, about ten feet high and a quarter of a mile long, probably the finest of its kind in England. So thick are the upper branches of the yew trees that, as William Cobbett writes, when he visited Albury in Mr. Drummond's time, they kept out both the rain and sun, and alike in summer and winter afford "a most delightful walk." The grand terrace under the hill, "thirty or forty feet wide, and a quarter of a mile long, of the finest green-sward, and as level as a die," particularly delighted him; and the careful way in which the fruit trees were protected from the wind, and the springs along the hill-side collected to water the garden, gratified his practical mind. "Take it altogether," he goes on, "this certainly is the prettiest garden that I ever beheld. There was taste and sound judgment at every step in the laying out of this place. Everywhere utility and convenience is combined with beauty. The terrace is by far the finest thing of the sort that I ever saw, and the whole thing altogether is a great compliment to the taste of the times in which it was formed." The honest old reformer's satisfaction in these gardens was increased by the reflection that the owner was worthy of his estate, seeing that he was famed for his justice and kindness towards the labouring classes—"who, God knows, have very few friends amongst the rich;" and adds, that he for one has no sympathy with "the fools" who want a revolution for the purpose of getting hold of other people's property. "There are others who like pretty gardens as well as I, and if the question were to be decided according to the laws of the strongest, or, as the French call it, *droit du plus fort*, my chance would be but a very poor one."

CHAPTER VI

SHERE TO REIGATE

THE Pilgrims' Way ran through Albury Park, passing close to the old church and under the famous yew hedge, and crossed the clear trout stream of the Tillingbourne by a ford still known as "Chantry Ford." Here a noble avenue of lime trees brings us to Shere church, a building as remarkable for the beauty of its situation as for its architectural interest. The lovely Early English doorway, the heavy transitional arches of the nave and the fourteenth-century chancel are still unhurt, and among the fragments of old glass we recognise the flax-breaker, which was the crest of the Brays, one of the oldest families in the county, who are, we rejoice to think, still represented here. Shere itself is one of the most charming villages in all this lovely neighbourhood. For many years now it has been a favourite resort of artistic and literary men, who find endless delight in the quiet beauty of the surrounding country. Subjects for pen and pencil abound in all directions; quaint old timbered houses, picturesque water-mills and barns, deep ferny lanes shaded by overhanging trees, and exquisite glimpses of heather-clad downs meet us at every turn. Fair as the scene is, travellers are seldom seen in these hilly regions; and so complete is the stillness, so pure the mountain air, that we might almost fancy ourselves in the heart of the Highlands, instead of thirty miles from town. Here it was, in the midst of the wild scenery of these Surrey Hills, that a sudden end closed the life of a great prelate of our own days, Samuel Wilberforce, Bishop of Winchester. A granite cross at Evershed's Rough, just below Lord Farrer's house at Abinger Hall, now marks the spot where his horse stumbled and fell as he rode down the hill towards Holmbury on that summer afternoon.

About a mile beyond Abinger we reach the home of John Evelyn, and see the grey tower of the church where he is buried. This is Wotton—the town of the woods, as he loved to call it—"sweetly environed" with "venerable woods and delicious streams;" Wotton where, after all his wanderings and all the turmoil of those troublous times, Evelyn found a peaceful haven wherein to end his days. There are the terraces, the "fountains and groves," in which he took delight; there, too, are the pine-woods which he planted, not only for ornament, and because they "create a perpetual spring," but because he held the air to be improved by their "odoriferous and balsamical emissions." Not only these trees, but the oak and ash, and all the different species which he studied so closely and has written about so well, were dear to him as his own children, and he speaks in pathetic language of the violent storm which blew down two thousand of his finest trees in a single night, and almost within sight of his dwelling, and left Wotton, "now no more Woodtonn, stripped and naked, and almost ashamed to own its name. Methinks that I still hear, and I am sure that I feel, the dismal groans of our forests, when that late dreadful hurricane, happening on the 26th of November, 1703, subverted so many thousands of goodly oaks, prostrating the trees, laying them in ghastly postures, like whole regiments fallen in battle by the sword of the conqueror, and crushing all that grew beneath them." Evelyn's descendants have bestowed the same care on the woods and plantations, and in spite of the havoc wrought by wind and tempest, Wotton is still remarkable for the beauty of its forest-trees and masses of flowering rhododendrons.

The red-brick house has been a good deal altered during the present century, but is still full of memorials of Evelyn. His portrait, and that of his wife and father-in-law, Sir Richard Browne, are there, and that of his "angelic friend," Mistress Blagge, the wife of Godolphin, whose beautiful memory he has enshrined in the pages of the little volume that bears her name. The drawings which he made on his foreign travels are there too; and better still, the books in which he took such pride and pleasure, carefully bound, bearing on their backs a device and motto which he chose, a spray of oak, palm, and olive entwined together, with the words, "Omnia explorate; meliora retinete." But the most precious relic of all is the Prayer Book used by Charles I. on the morning of his execution. It was saved from destruction by a devoted loyalist, Isaac Herault, brother of a Walloon minister in London, and afterwards given by him to Evelyn's father-in-law, Sir Richard Browne. The fly-leaf bears a Latin inscription with this note:—This is the Booke which Charles the First, *Martyr beatus*, did use upon the Scaffold, XXXJan., 1649, being the Day of his glorious martyrdom."

The exact course of the Pilgrims' Way here is uncertain. After leaving Shere church it disappears, and we must climb a steep lane past Gomshall station, to find the track again on Hackhurst Downs. The line of yews is to be seen at intervals all along these downs, and as we descend into the valley of the Mole, opposite the heights of Box Hill, we pass four venerable yew trees standing in a field by themselves. One of the group was struck by lightning many years ago, but still stretches its gaunt, withered arms against the sky, like some weather-beaten sign-post marking the way to Canterbury.

The town of Dorking lies in the break here made in the chalk hills by the passage of the river Mole; Milton's "sullen Mole that windeth underground," or, as Spenser sings in his "Faërie Queen,"—

"Mole, that like a mousling mole doth make

His way still underground, till Thames he overtake."

The Mole owes its fame to the fact that it is so seldom seen, and several of the swallows or gullies into which it disappears at intervals along its chalky bed are at Burford, close to Dorking. The ponds which supplied the perch for that *water-sousie* which Dutch merchants came to eat at Dorking, are still to be seen in the fields under Redhill, and near them many an old timbered house and mill-wheel well worth painting.

To-day Dorking is a quiet, sleepy little place, but its situation on the Stane Street, the great Roman road from Chichester to London, formerly made it a centre of considerable importance, and the size and excellence of the old-fashioned inns still bear witness to its departed grandeur. Whether, as seems most probable, the old road ran under the wall of Denbies Park, and across the gap now made by the Dorking lime works, or whether, as the Ordnance map indicates, it crossed the breezy heights of Ranmore Common, pilgrims to Canterbury certainly crossed the Mole at Burford Bridge about half a mile from the town. The remains of an ancient shrine known as the Pilgrims' Chapel are still shown in Westhumble Lane. The path itself bears the name of Paternoster Lane, and the fields on either side are called the Pray Meadows. From this point the path runs along under Boxhill, the steep down that rises abruptly on the eastern side of Dorking, and takes its name from the box-trees which here spring up so plentifully in the smooth green turf above the chalk. Boxhill is, we all know, one of the chief attractions which Dorking offers to Londoners. The other is to be found in the fine parks of Deepdene and Betchworth, immediately adjoining the town. The famous gardens and art collections of Deepdene, and the noble lime avenue of Betchworth, which now forms part of the same estate, have often been visited and described. The house at Deepdene is now closed to the public, but the traveller can still stroll under the grand old trees on the river bank, and enjoy a wealthy variety of forest scenery almost unrivalled in England. A picturesque bridge over the Mole leads back to the downs on the opposite side of the valley, where the old track pursues its way along the lower slope of the hills, often wending its course through ploughed fields and tangled thickets and disappearing altogether in places where chalk quarries and lime works have cut away the face of the down. But on the whole the line of yews which mark the road is more regular between Dorking and Reigate than in its earlier course, and at Buckland, a village two miles west of Reigate, a whole procession of these trees descends into the valley.

All this part of the road is rich in Roman remains. Of these one of the most interesting was the building discovered in 1875, at Colley Farm, in the parish of Reigate, just south of the Way. Not only were several cinerary urns and fragments of Roman pottery dug up, but the walls of a Roman building were found under those of the present farmhouse. Some twenty years ago a similar building was discovered at Abinger, also in the immediate vicinity of the track, but unfortunately it was completely destroyed in the absence of the owner, Sir Thomas Farrer. Another Roman house came to light in 1813, at Bletchingley, and one chamber, which appeared to be a hypocaust, was excavated at the time. Lastly, considerable Roman remains have been discovered and carefully excavated by Mr. Leveson-Gower in the park at Titsey. Of these the most important are a Roman villa, which was thoroughly excavated in 1864, together with a group of larger buildings, apparently the farm belonging to the ancient house. These are only a few of the principal links in the chain of Roman buildings which lie along the course of this ancient trackway, and which all help to prove its importance as a thoroughfare at the time of the Roman occupation.

Another point of interest regarding this part of the Pilgrims' Way is its connection with John Bunyan. When his peculiar opinions and open-air preachings had brought him into trouble with the authorities, he came to hide in these Surrey hills, and earned his living for some time as a travelling tinker. Two houses, one at Horn Hatch, on Shalford Common, the other at Quarry Hill, in Guildford, are still pointed out as having been inhabited by him at this time; and a recent writer has suggested that in all probability the recollections of Pilgrimage days, then fresh in the minds of the people, first gave him the idea of his "Pilgrim's Progress." Certainly more than one incident in the history of the road bears a close resemblance to the tale of Christian's adventures. Thus, for instance, the swampy marshes at Shalford may have been the Slough of Despond, the blue Surrey hills seen from the distance may well have seemed to him the Delectable Mountains, and the name of Doubting Castle actually exists at a point of the road near Box Hill. Lastly, the great fair at Shalford corresponds exactly with Bunyan's description of Vanity Fair, no newly erected business, but "a thing of ancient standing," where "the ware of Rome and her merchandise is greatly promoted ... only our

English nation have taken a dislike thereat." In the days when Bunyan wrote, the annual fair had degenerated into a lawless and noisy assembly, where little trade was done, and much drinking and fighting and rude horseplay went on, as he may have found to his cost. The wares of Rome, in fact, were commodities no longer in fashion, and soon the fair itself came to an end and passed away, like so many other things that had been called into being by the Canterbury Pilgrimage.

CHAPTER VII

REIGATE TO CHEVENING

ALTHOUGH the town of Reigate lies in the valley, it certainly takes its name from the Pilgrims' Road to Canterbury. In Domesday it is called Cherchfelle, and it is not till the latter part of the twelfth century that the comparatively modern name of Rigegate, the Ridge Road, was applied, first of all to the upper part of the parish, and eventually to the whole town. In those days a chapel dedicated to the memory of the blessed martyr, St. Thomas, stood at the east end of the long street, on a site now occupied by a market-house, built early in the last century, and part of the ancient foundations of this pilgrimage shrine were brought to light when the adjoining prison was enlarged some eighty or ninety years back. Another chapel, dedicated to St. Laurence the Martyr, stood farther down the street; and a third, the Chapel of Holy Cross, belonged to the Augustine Canons of the Priory founded by William of Warrenne, Earl of Surrey, in the thirteenth century. In Saxon days Reigate, or Holm Castle, as it was then termed, from its situation at the head of the valley of Holmesdale, was an important stronghold, and the vigour and persistence with which the incursions of the Danes were repelled by the inhabitants of this district gave rise to the rhyme quoted by Camden—

"The Vale of Holmesdale
Never wonne, ne never shall."

At the Conquest the manor was granted to William of Warrenne, and from that time the castle became the most powerful fortress of the mighty Earls of Surrey. In the days of John it shared the fate of Guildford Castle, and was one of the strongholds which opened its gates to Louis VIII., King of France, on his march from the Kentish Coast to Winchester. The Fitzalans succeeded the Warrennes in the possession of Reigate, and in the reign of Edward VI., both the castle and the Priory were granted to the Howards of Effingham. Queen Elizabeth's Lord High Admiral, the victor of the Invincible Armada, lies buried in the vault under the chancel of Reigate Church. In Stuart times the castle gradually fell into decay, until it was finally destroyed by order of Parliament, during the Civil War, lest it should fall into the King's hands. Now only the mound of the ancient keep remains, and some spacious subterranean chambers which may have served as cellars or dungeons in Norman times. The Priory has also been replaced by a modern house, and is the property of Lady Henry Somerset, the representative of the Earl Somers, to whom William III. granted Reigate in 1697.

Reigate is frequently mentioned in Cobbett's "Rural Rides," and it was the sight of the Priory that set him moralising over monasteries and asking himself if, instead of being, as we take it for granted, *bad things*, they were not, after all, better than *poor-rates*, and if the monks and nuns, who *fed the poor*, were not more to be commended than the rich pensioners of the State, who *feed upon the poor*.

Close to this ancient foundation is the hilly common known as Reigate Park, a favourite haunt with artists, who find endless subjects in the fern-grown dells and romantic hollows, the clumps of thorn-trees with their gnarled stems and spreading boughs, their wealth of wild flowers and berries. The views over Reigate itself and the Priory grounds on one side, and over the Sussex Weald on the other, are very charming; but a still finer prospect awaits us on the North Downs on the opposite side of the valley, where the Pilgrims' Road goes on its course. The best way is to climb Reigate Hill as far as the suspension bridge, and follow a path cut in the chalk to the summit of the ridge. It leads through a beechwood on to the open downs, where, if the day is clear, one of the finest views in the whole of England—in the whole world, says Cobbett—breaks upon us. The Weald of Surrey and of Sussex, from the borders of Hampshire to the ridge of East Grinstead, and Crowborough Beacon, near Tunbridge Wells, lies spread out at our feet. Eastward, the eye ranges over the Weald of Kent and the heights above Sevenoaks; westward the purple ridge of Leith Hill and the familiar crest of Hindhead meet us; and far away to the south are the Brighton downs and Chanctonbury Ring.

The line of yew trees appears again here, and after keeping along the top of the ridge for about a mile, the Pilgrims' Way enters Gatton Park, and passing through the woods near Lord Oxenbridge's house, joins the avenue that leads to Merstham. Gatton itself, which, like Reigate, takes its name from the Pilgrims' Road—Saxon, Gatetun, the town of the road —was chiefly famous for the electoral privileges which it so long enjoyed. From the time of Henry VI. until the Reform Bill of 1832, this very small borough returned two members to Parliament. In the reign of Henry VIII. Sir Roger Copley is described as the burgess and sole inhabitant of the borough and town of Gatton, and for many years the constituency consisted of one person, the lord of the manor.

At the beginning of the present century there were only eight houses in the whole parish, a fact which naturally roused the ire of William Cobbett. "Before you descend the hill to go into Reigate," he writes in one of his Rural Rides, "you pass Gatton, which is a very rascally spot of earth." And when rainy weather detained him a whole day at Reigate, he moralises in this vein—"*In* one rotten borough, one the most rotten too, and with another still more rotten *up upon the hill*, in Reigate and close by Gatton, how can I help reflecting, how can my mind be otherwise than filled with reflections on the marvellous deeds of the collective wisdom of the nation?" These privileges doubled the value of the property, and when Lord Monson bought Gatton Park in 1830, he paid a hundred thousand pounds for the place; but the days of close boroughs were already numbered, and less than two years afterwards the Reform Bill deprived Gatton of both its members. The little town hall of Gatton, where the important ceremony of electing two representatives to serve in Parliament was performed, is still standing, an interesting relic of bygone days, on a mound in the park, almost hidden by large chestnut trees.

Gatton House is chiefly remarkable for the marble hall built by the same Lord Monson in imitation of the Orsini Chapel at Rome, and adorned with rich marbles which he had brought from Italy. The collection of pictures, formed by the same nobleman, contains several good Dutch and Italian pictures, including the "Vierge au bas-relief," a graceful Holy Family, which takes its name from a small carved tablet in the background. It was long held to be an early work by the great Leonardo da Vinci, and was purchased by Lord Monson of Mr. Woodburn for £4,000, but is now generally attributed to his pupil, Cesare da Sesto.

Like so many of the churches we have already mentioned, like Seale and Wanborough, and the chapels of St. Katherine and St. Martha, like the old church at Titsey and the present one at Chevening, Gatton was originally a Pilgrims' church. Now it has little that is old to show, for it was restored by Lord Monson in 1831, and adorned with a variety of treasures from all parts of the Continent. The stained glass comes from the monastery of Aerschot, near Louvain, the altar-rails from Tongres, the finely carved choir-stalls and canopies from Ghent, and the altar and pulpit from Nuremberg. Like most of the mediæval wood-work and glass which has come to England from that "Quaint old town of toil and traffic, Quaint old town of art and song," these last are said to have been designed by the great master of the Franconian city, Albert Dürer.

The Pilgrims' Way, as has been already said, runs through Gatton Park, and brings us out close to Merstham, and through lanes shaded with fine oaks and beeches we reach the pretty little village, with its old timbered cottages and still older church buried in the woods. Local writers of the last century frequently allude to the Pilgrims' Road as passing through this parish, although its exact course is not easy to trace. It seems, however, certain that the track passed near Lord Hylton's house, and south of the church, which stands close by. In mediæval times, Merstham formed part of the vast estates held by the monks of Christ Church, Canterbury, and was bestowed upon them by Athelstan, a son of Ethelred the Unready, in the tenth century. There was a church here at the time of the Norman Conquest, but the only portion of the present building dating from that period is a fine old square Norman font which, like several others in the neighbourhood, is of Sussex marble. Of later date, there is much that is extremely interesting. The tower and the west door are Early English, and the chancel arch is adorned with curious acanthus-leaf mouldings, while the porch and chancel are Late Perpendicular.

After passing Merstham Church the track is lost in a medley of roads and railway cuttings, but soon the line of yews appears again, climbing the crest of the hill, and can be followed for some distance along White Hill, or Quarry Hangers, as these downs are commonly called. The next object of interest which it passes is the War Camp, or Cardinal's Cap, as it is sometimes termed, an old British earthwork on the face of the chalk escarpment. Then the path turns into a wood, and we leave it to descend on Godstone. This is a fascinating spot for artists. The low irregular houses are grouped round a spacious green and goose-pond, shaded by fine horse-chestnuts, and there is a charming inn, the White Hart or Clayton Arms, with gabled front and large bay-windows of the good old-fashioned type. "A beautiful village," wrote Cobbett, ninety years ago, "chiefly of one street, with a fine large green before it, and with a pond in the green;" and he goes on to speak of the neatness of the gardens and of the double violets, "as large as small pinks," which grew in the garden of this same inn, and of which the landlady was good enough to give some roots. Happily for his peace of mind, he adds, "The vile rotten borough of Bletchingley, which lies under the downs close by, is out of sight."

From Godstone it is a pleasant walk over the open commons, along the top of the ridge, looking over the Weald of Sussex and across the valleys of Sevenoaks and Tunbridge to the Kentish hills. Once more we track the line of the Pilgrims' Way as it emerges from the woods above the Godstone quarries and, passing under Winder's Hill and by Marden Park, reaches a wood called Palmers Wood. The name is significant, more especially since there is no record of any owner who bore that name. Here its course is very clearly defined, and when, in the autumn of 1890, pipes for carrying water out of the hill were laid down, a section of the old paved road was cut across. A little farther on, at Limpsfield Lodge Farm, just on the edge of Titsey park, it formed the farm road till 1875.

At this point the path was ten feet wide, and the original hedges remained. Before entering the park of Titsey, the way runs through part of Oxted parish, where a spring still bears the name of St. Thomas's Well, and then reaches Titsey Place.

Few places in this part of Surrey are more attractive than this old home of the Greshams. The purity of the air, praised by Aubrey long ago for its sweet, delicate, and wholesome virtues, the health-giving breezes of the surrounding downs and commons, the natural loveliness of the place, and the taste with which the park and gardens have been laid out, all help to make Titsey a most delightful spot. Its beautiful woods stretch along the grassy slopes of Botley Hill, and the clump of trees on the heights known as Cold-harbour Green is 881 feet above the sea, and marks the loftiest point in the whole range of the North Downs. Wherever the eye rests, one ridge of wooded hill after the other seems to rise and melt away into the soft blue haze. Nor is there any lack of other attractions to invite the attention of scholar and antiquary. The place is full of historic associations. A whole wealth of antiquities, coins, urns, and pottery, have been dug up in the park, and some remains of Roman buildings were discovered there a few years ago, close to the Pilgrims' Way. After the conquest Titsey was given to the great Earls of Clare, who owned the property at the time of the Domesday Survey. In the fourteenth century it belonged to the Uvedale family, and two hundred years later was sold to Sir John Gresham, an uncle of Sir Thomas Gresham, the illustrious merchant of Queen Elizabeth's court, and the founder of the Royal Exchange. A fine portrait of Sir Thomas himself, by Antonio More, now hangs in the library of Titsey Place. Unfortunately the Greshams suffered for their loyalty to Charles I., and after the death of the second Sir Marmaduke Gresham in 1742, a large part of the property was sold. His son, Sir John, succeeded in partly retrieving the fortunes of the family, and rebuilt and enlarged the old manor-house, which had been allowed to fall into a ruinous state. But the Tudor arches of the east wing still remain, as well as much of the fine oak panelling which adorned its walls; and the crest of the Greshams, a grasshopper, may still be seen in the hall chimney-piece. The present owner, Mr. Leveson-Gower, is a lineal descendant of the last baronet, and inherited Titsey from his great-grandmother Katherine, the heiress of the Greshams. The fourteenth-century church was unluckily pulled down a hundred years ago, because Sir John Gresham thought it stood too near his own house, but an old yew in the garden and some tombstones of early Norman date still mark its site. The course of the Pilgrims' Way through the Park is clearly marked by a double row of fine ash trees, and the flint stones with which the road itself is paved may still be seen under the turf. Further along the road is a very old farmhouse, which was formerly a hostelry, and still bears the name of the Pilgrims' Lodge. From Titsey the Way runs along the side of the hills, under Tatsfield Church, which stands on the summit of the ridge, and about a mile above the pretty little towns of Westerham and Brasted. Here the boundary of the counties is crossed, and the traveller enters Kent. Soon we reach the gates of Chevening Park, where, as at Titsey, the Pilgrims' Way formerly passed very near the house, until it was closed by Act of Parliament in 1780.

The manor of Chevening, originally the property of the See of Canterbury, was held in the thirteenth and fourteenth centuries by the family of Chevening, from whence it passed to the Lennards, who became Barons Dacre and Earls of Sussex. In the last century it was bought by General Stanhope, the distinguished soldier and statesman, who, after reducing the island of Minorca, served King George I. successively as Secretary of State and First Lord of the Treasury. Inigo Jones built the house for Richard Lennard, Lord Dacre, early in the seventeenth century, but since then it has undergone such extensive alterations that little of the original structure remains, and the chief interest lies in a valuable collection of historical portraits, including those of the Chesterfields, Stanhopes, and the great Lord Chatham. The last-named statesman, whose daughter Hester married Charles, Lord Stanhope, in 1774, was a frequent visitor at Chevening, and is said to have planned the beautiful drive which leads through the woods north of the house to the top of the downs. The little village of Chevening lies on the other side of the park, just outside Lord Stanhope's gates and close to the old church of St. Botolph, which was one of the shrines frequented by the pilgrims on their way to Canterbury. There are some good Early English arches in the nave and chancel, and a western tower of Perpendicular date. The south chapel contains many imposing sepulchral monuments to the different lords of the manor. Amongst them are those of John Lennard, who was sheriff of the county and held several offices under the crown in the reigns of Henry VIII. and Elizabeth, and of his son Sampson, who with his wife Margaret, Lady Dacre in her own right, reposes under a sumptuous canopy of alabaster surrounded by kneeling effigies of their children. There is also a fine black marble monument to the memory of James, Earl of Stanhope, the prime minister of George I., who was buried here with great pomp in 1721. He was actually in office at the time of his death, and was taken ill in the House of Lords, and breathed his last the next day. But the most beautiful tomb here is Chantrey's effigy of Lady Frederica Stanhope sleeping with her babe in her arms, and an expression of deep content and peace upon her quiet face.

"Storms may rush in, and crimes and woes
Deform the quiet bower;
They may not mar the deep repose
Of that immortal flower."

CHAPTER VIII

OTFORD TO WROTHAM

WE have followed the Pilgrims' Way over Hampshire Downs and Surrey hills and commons, through the woods which Evelyn planted, and along the ridge where Cobbett rode. We have seen the track become overgrown with tangled shrubs and underwood, and disappear altogether in places. We have lost the road at one point in the fields, to find it again half a mile further; we have noted the regular lines of yews climbing up the hill-side, and the lonely survivors which are left standing bare and desolate in the middle of the corn-fields. The part of the ancient road on which we are now entering differs in several important respects from its earlier course. From the time the Pilgrims' Way enters Kent its track is clearly marked. Already we have followed its line through Titsey and along the downs as far as Chevening, where the path, now closed, may be traced through Lord Stanhope's Park. A group of magnificent old yew trees arrests our attention just beyond Chevening, before the road from Sevenoaks to Bromley is crossed. Then the Way descends into the valley of the Darent, an excellent trout-stream which flows north through this chalk district to join the Thames near Dartford, and after crossing the ford over that river, regains the hills at Otford. From this place it runs along under the hill in one unbroken line all the way to Eastwell Park, between Ashford and Canterbury. It is a good bridle-way, somewhat grass-grown in places, in others enclosed by hedges, and still used by farmers for their carts. Before toll-bars were abolished there was a good deal of traffic along this part of the Pilgrims' Road, which, running as it does parallel with the turnpike road along the valley to Ashford, was much used as a means of evading the payment of toll. This cause is now removed, and excepting for an occasional hunting-man who makes use of the soft track along the hill-side, or a camp of gipsies sitting round their fire, waggoners and ploughmen are the only wayfarers to be met with along the Pilgrims' Road. But the old name still clings to the track, and as long as the squires of Kent have any respect for the traditions of the past, any particle of historic sense remaining, they will not allow the Pilgrims' Way to be wiped out.

In actual beauty of scenery this portion of the Way may not equal the former part. We miss the wild loveliness of Surrey commons, the rare picturesqueness of the rolling downs round Guildford and Dorking, but this Kentish land has a charm of its own, which grows upon you the longer you know it. These steep slopes and wooded hollows, these grand old church towers and quaint village streets, these homesteads with their vast barns of massive timber and tall chimney-stacks overshadowed with oaks and beeches, cannot fail to delight the eyes of all who find pleasure in rural scenes. And all along our way we have that noble prospect over the wide plains of the dim blue Weald, which is seldom absent from our eyes, as we follow this narrow track up and down the rugged hill-side. In historic interest and precious memorials of the past, this part of the Pilgrims' Way, we need hardly say, is surpassingly rich. Endless are the great names and stirring events which these scenes recall: battlefields where memorable fights were fought in days long ago, churches and lands that were granted to the Archbishops or Abbots of Canterbury before the Conquest, manor-houses which our kings and queens have honoured with their presence in the days of yore. All these things, and many more of equal interest and renown, will the traveller find as he follows the Pilgrims' Way along the chalk hills which form the backbone of Kent.

The first resting-place which the pilgrims would find on this part of their route would be the Archbishop's manor-house at Otford. There were no less than fifteen of these episcopal residences in different parts of Kent, Surrey, and Sussex, and of these, three lay along the Kentish portion of the Pilgrims' Way. The palace at Otford possessed an especial sanctity in the eyes of wayfarers journeying to the shrine of St. Thomas, as having been a favourite residence of the martyred Archbishop himself. The manor was originally granted to the See of Canterbury in 791, by Offa, king of Mercia, who defeated Aldric, king of Kent, at Otford in 773, and conquered almost the whole province.

More than two hundred years later, Otford was the scene of another battle, in which Edmund Ironside defeated the Danes under Knut, and to this day bones are dug up in the meadow which bears the name of Danefield. From the tenth century the Archbishops had a house here, and Otford is described in the Domesday Survey as *Terra Archiepi Cantuariensis*. So it remained until Cranmer surrendered the palace, with many other of his possessions, to Henry VIII. The mediæval Archbishops seem to have had an especial affection for Otford, and spent much of their time at this pleasant country seat. Archbishop Winchelsea entertained Edward I. in 1300, and was living here at the time of his death thirteen years later, when his remains were borne by the King's command to Canterbury, and buried there with great state. Simon Islip enclosed the park, and Archbishop Deane repaired the walls; but the whole was rebuilt on a grander scale by Warham, who spent upwards of thirty thousand pounds upon the house, and received Henry VIII. here several times in the first years of his reign.

After Otford had become Crown property, the Archbishop's manor-house passed into the hands of the Sydneys and Smyths, who dismantled the castle, as it was then commonly called, and allowed the walls to fall into ruin. Two massive octagonal towers of three stories, with double square-headed windows, and a fragment of a cloister, now used as farm stables, are the only portions remaining. These evidently formed part of the outer court, and are good specimens of fifteenth-century brickwork. The tower was considerably higher a hundred years ago, and Hasted describes the ruins as covering nearly an acre of ground. The stones of the structure were largely used in the neighbouring buildings, and the Bull Inn contains a good deal of fine oak wainscoting, and several handsome carved mantelpieces, which originally belonged to the castle. Two heads in profile, carved in oak over one of the fireplaces, are said to represent Henry VIII. and Katherine of Aragon. A bath, or chamber, paved and lined with stone, about thirty feet long, and ten or twelve feet deep, not far from the ruins, still bears the name of Becket's Well. Tradition ascribes the birth of the spring which supplies it to St. Thomas, who, finding no water at Otford, struck the hill-side with his staff, and at once brought forth a clear stream, which since then has never been known to fail. Another legend tells how the Saint one day, being "busie at his prayers in the garden at Otford, was much disturbed by the sweete note and melodie of a nightingale that sang in a bush beside him, and in the might of his holinesse commanded all birds of this kind to be henceforth silent," after which the nightingale was never heard at Otford. But with the decay of the palace and the departure of the Archbishops, the spell was broken; and the Protestant Lambarde, when he was at Otford, takes pleasure in recording how many nightingales he heard singing thereabouts.

From Otford the Pilgrims' Way runs along the edge of the hills about half a mile above the villages of Kemsing and Wrotham, and passes close to St. Clere, a mansion built by Inigo Jones, where Mrs. Boscawen, the witty correspondent of Mrs. Delany and the friend of Johnson and Boswell, was born. Kemsing still retains its old church and well, both consecrated to the memory of the Saxon Princess, St. Edith, whose image in the churchyard was, during centuries, the object of the peasants' devout veneration. "Some seelie bodie," writes Lambarde, who visited these shrines in Queen Elizabeth's reign, and delights in pouring contempt on the old traditions of these country shrines, "brought a peche or two, or a bushelle of corne, to the churche after praiers made, offered it to the image of the saint. Of this offering the priest used to toll the greatest portion, and then to take one handful or little more of the residue (for you must consider he woulde bee sure to gaine by the bargaine), the which, after aspersion of holy water and the mumbling of a fewe words of conjuration, he first dedicated to the image of Saint Edith, and then delivered it backe to the partie that brought it; who departed with full persuasion that if he mingled that hallowed handfull with his seede corne, it would preserve from harme and prosper in growthe the whole heape that he should sowe, were it never so great a stacke."

Wrotham was the site of another of the Archbishops' manor-houses, and rivalled Otford in antiquity, having been granted to the See of Canterbury by Athelstan in 964. Wrotham was never as favourite a residence with the Archbishops as Otford, but they stopped here frequently on their progresses through Kent, until, in the fourteenth century, Simon Islip pulled down the house to supply materials for the building of his new palace at Maidstone. A terrace and some scanty remains of the offices are the only fragments now to be seen at Wrotham, but the charming situation of the village in the midst of luxuriant woods, and the beauty of the view over the Weald from Wrotham Hill, attract many visitors. The church has several features of architectural interest, including a handsome rood-screen of the fourteenth century, and a watching-chamber over the chancel, as well as a curious archway under the tower, which was probably used as a passage for processions from the Palace. It contains many tombs and brasses, chiefly of the Peckham family, who held the manor of Yaldham in this parish for upwards of five hundred years. Below the church is Wrotham Place, a fine old Tudor house with a corridor and rooms of the fifteenth century, and a charming garden front bearing the date 1560. Fairlawn, the ancestral home of the Vanes, also lies in a corner of Wrotham parish, and a terrace, bordered with close-clipped yew hedges, and surrounded by sunny lawns, where peacocks spread their tails over the grass, is still pointed out as a favourite walk of that stout old regicide, Sir Harry Vane. Ightham, with its famous Mote, so perfect a picture of an old English house, is close by, within a walk of Wrotham station, but lies, unluckily, on the opposite side from the line of hills along which our path takes us.

CHAPTER IX

WROTHAM TO HOLLINGBOURNE

THE Pilgrims' Way continues its course over Wrotham Hill and along the side of the chalk downs. This part of the track is a good bridle road, with low grass banks or else hedges on either side, and commands fine views over the rich Kentish plains, the broad valley of the Medway, and the hills on the opposite shore. The river itself glitters in the sun, but as we draw nearer the beauty of the prospect is sorely marred by the ugly chimneys and dense smoke of the Snodland limestone works.

At one point on the downs, close to the Vigo Inn, a few hundred yards above our road, there is a very extensive view over the valley of the Thames, ranging from Shooters' Hill to Gravesend, and far away out to sea. In the daytime the masts of the shipping in the river are clearly seen. At night the Nore lights twinkle like stars in the distance. The height of these downs is close on 700 feet, that of Knockholt is 783 feet. On the other side of the Medway the chalk range is considerably lower, and the highest points are above Detling, 657 feet, Hollingbourne, 606 feet, and Charing, 640 feet.

The Way now runs past Pilgrims' house, formerly the Kentish Drovers' Inn, above the old church and village of Trottescliffe (Trosley) and the megalithic stones known as Coldrum circle, one of the best preserved cromlechs along the road. Further on a short lane leads south to Birling Place, the ancient home of the Nevills, who have owned the estate since the middle of the fifteenth century, while in a group of old farm buildings at Paddlesworth (formerly Paulsford) we find the remains of a Norman Pilgrims' Chapel, with a fine Early English arch. The track now crosses a large field and enters Snodland, an old town containing many Roman remains, and an interesting church, but sadly disfigured by cement works and paper factories.

Here the pilgrims left the hills to descend into the valley below. Twice before, at Shalford and Dorking, they had crossed the rivers which make their way through the chalk range; now they had reached the third great break in the downs, and the broad stream of the Medway lay at their feet. They might, if they pleased, go on to Rochester, three miles higher up, and join the road taken by the London pilgrims along the Watling Street to Canterbury—the route of Chaucer's pilgrimage. But most of them, it appears, preferred to follow the hills to which they had clung so long.

The exact point where they crossed the river has been often disputed. According to the old maps it was by the ford at Cuxton, where the river was shallow enough to allow of their passage. From Bunker's Farm, immediately above Birling, a road diverges northwards to Cuxton and Rochester, and was certainly used by many of the pilgrims. At Upper Halling, on this track, we may still see the lancet windows of a pilgrims' shrine formerly dedicated to St. Laurence, which have been built into some cottages known as Chapel houses. The Bishops of Rochester, who held this manor from Egbert's days, had "a right fair house" at Lower Halling, on the banks of the Medway, with a vineyard which produced grapes for King Henry III.'s table. This pleasant manor-house on the river was the favourite summer residence of Bishop Hamo de Hethe, who built a new hall and chapel in the reign of Edward I., and placed his own statue on a gateway which was still standing in the eighteenth century. Another interesting house, Whorne Place, lies a little higher up, on the banks of the Medway, where the grass-grown track leading from Bunker's Farm joins the main road to Cuxton and Rochester. This fine brick mansion formerly belonged to the Levesons, and the quarterings of Sir John Leveson and his two wives are to be seen above the central porch.

In the thirteenth century a great number of pilgrims seem to have stopped at Maidstone, where, in 1261, Archbishop Boniface built a hospital for their reception on the banks of the Medway. The funds which supported this hospital, the Newark—New-work, Novi operis, as it was called— were diverted by Archbishop Courtenay, a hundred and forty years later, to the maintenance of his new college of All Saints, on the opposite side of the river, but a remnant of the older foundation is still preserved in the beautiful Early English Chancel of St. Peter's Church, which was originally attached to Boniface's hospital, and is still known as the Pilgrims' Chapel. By the time that Archbishop Courtenay founded his college, the stream of pilgrims had greatly diminished, and the hostel which had been intended for their resting-place was rapidly sinking into a common almshouse. Maidstone, too, no doubt, lay considerably out of the pilgrims' course, and the great majority naturally preferred to cross the Medway by the ferry at Snodland. Others again might choose Aylesford, which lay a mile or two below. At this ancient town, the Eglesford of the Saxon Chronicle, there was a stone bridge across the river, and a Carmelite Priory founded in 1240 by Richard de Grey, on his return from the Crusades, where the pilgrims would be sure to find shelter. But even if they did not cross the Medway at this place, where the old church stands so picturesquely on its high bank overhanging river and red roofs, the pilgrims certainly passed through the parish of Aylesford. For on the opposite banks of the ferry at Snodland the familiar line of yew trees appears again, ascending the hill by Burham church, and runs through the upper part of Aylesford parish, close to the famous dolmen of Kits Coty House. This most interesting sepulchral monument, Kêd-coit—Celtic for the Tomb in the Wood—consists of three upright blocks of sandstone about eight feet high and eight feet broad, with a covering stone of eleven feet which forms the roof, and is one of a group of similar remains which lie scattered over the hill-side and are locally known as the Countless Stones. We have here, in fact, a great cemetery of the Druids which once extended for many miles on both sides of the river. Deep pits dug out in the chalk, filled with flints and covered with slabs of stone, have been discovered on Aylesford Common, and a whole avenue of stones formerly connected this burial place with the cromlechs at Addington, six miles off. Here, if the old legend be true, was fought the great battle which decided the fate of Britain, and gave England into the hands of the English. For at this place, the old chroniclers say, about the year 455, the Saxon invaders stopped on their march to the Castle of Rochester, and turning southwards met the Britons in that deadly fray, when both Kentigern and Horsa were left dead on the field of battle. Ancient military entrenchments are still visible on the hill-side near Kits Coty House, and a boulder on the top was long pointed out as the stone on which Hengist was proclaimed the first king of Kent.

About a mile from this memorable spot, in the plains at the foot of the downs, was a shrine which no pilgrim of mediæval days would leave unvisited, the Cistercian Abbey of Boxley, then generally known as the Abbatia S. Crucis de Gracias, the Abbey of the Holy Rood of Grace.

Not only was Boxley, next to Waverley Abbey, the oldest Cistercian house founded on this side of the Channel, the *filia propria* of the great house of Clairvaux, but the convent church rejoiced in the possession of two of the most celebrated wonder-working relics in all England. There was the image of St. Rumbold, that infant child of a Saxon prince who proclaimed himself a Christian the moment of his birth, and after three days spent in edifying his pagan hearers, departed this life. This image could only be lifted by the pure and good, and having a hidden spring, which could be worked by the hands or feet of the monks, was chiefly influenced by the amount of the coin that was paid into their hands. And there was that still greater marvel, the miraculous Rood, or winking image, a wooden crucifix which rolled its eyes and moved its lips in response to the devotees who crowded from all parts of England to see the wondrous sight. The clever mechanism of this image, said to have been invented by an English prisoner during his captivity in France, was exposed by Henry VIII.'s commissioners in 1538, who discovered "certayn ingyns of old wyer with olde roten stykkes in the back of the same," and showed them to the people of Maidstone on market-day, after which the Rood of Grace was taken to London and solemnly broken in pieces at Paul's Cross. The Abbey of Boxley owned vast lands, and the Abbots were frequently summoned to Parliament, and lived in great state. Among the royal guests whom they entertained was King Edward II., whose visit was made memorable by the letter which he addressed from Boxley Abbey to the Aldermen of the City of London, granting them the right of electing a Lord Mayor. At one time their extravagance brought them to the verge of ruin, as we learn from a letter which Archbishop Warham addressed to Cardinal Wolsey; but at the dissolution the Commissioners could find no cause of complaint against the monks, excepting the profusion of flowers in the convent garden, which made them comment on the waste of turning "the rents of the monastery into gillyflowers and roses." The foundations of the church where the Cistercians showed off their "sotelties" may still be traced in the gardens of the house built by Sir Thomas Wyatt on the site of the abbey. Here some precious fragments of the ruins are still preserved. The chapel of St. Andrew, which stood near the great gateway, has been turned into cottages, and the noble "guesten-house," where strangers were lodged, is now a barn. The old wall remains to show the once vast extent of the Abbey precincts. Now these grey stones are mantled with thick bushes of ivy, and a fine clump of elm trees overshadows the red-tiled roof of the ancient guest-house in the meadows, but we look in vain for poor Abbot John's gillyflowers and roses.

Between Boxley Abbey and Maidstone stretches the wide common of Penenden Heath, famous from time immemorial as the place where all great county meetings were held. Here the Saxons held their "gemotes," and here in 1076, was that memorable assembly before which Lanfranc pleaded the cause of the Church of Canterbury against Odo, Bishop of Bayeux, Earl of Kent, the Conqueror's half-brother, who had defrauded Christ Church of her rights, and laid violent hands on many of her manors and lands. Not only were the Kentish nobles and bishops summoned to try the cause, but barons and distinguished ecclesiastics, and many men "of great and good account," from all parts of England and Normandy, were present that day. Godfrey, Bishop of Coutances, represented the King, and Agelric, the aged Bishop of Chester, "an ancient man well versed in the laws and customs of the realm," was brought there in a chariot by the King's express command. Three days the trial lasted, during which Lanfranc pleaded his cause so well against the rapacious Norman that the see of Canterbury recovered its former possessions, and saw its liberties firmly established.

The village and church of Boxley (Bose-leu in Domesday), so called from the box trees that grow freely along the downs, as at Box Hill, are about a mile and a half beyond the Abbey, and lie on the sloping ground at the foot of the hills, close to the Pilgrims' Way. Old houses and timbered barns, with lofty gables and irregular roofs, are grouped round the church, which is itself as picturesque an object as any, with its massive towers and curious old red-tiled Galilee porch. Next we reach Detling, a small village, prettily situated on the slope of the hills, with a church containing a rare specimen of mediæval wood-work in the shape of a carved oak reading-desk, enriched with pierced tracery of the Decorated period. We pass Thurnham, with the foundations of its Saxon castle high up on the downs, and then enter Hollingbourne. As Boxley reminds us of the box trees on the hill-side, and Thurnham of the thorn trees in the wood, so Hollingbourne owes its name to the hollies on the burn or stream which runs through the parish. William Cobbett, whose memory has followed us all the way from the Itchen valley, describes how he rode over Hollingbourne Hill on his return from Dover to the Wen, and from the summit of that down, one of the highest in this neighbourhood, looked down over the fair Kentish land, which in its richness and beauty seemed to him another Garden of Eden.

CHAPTER X

HOLLINGBOURNE TO LENHAM

THE village of Hollingbourne lies at the foot of the hill, and an old inn at the corner of the Pilgrims' Road, now called the King's Head, was formerly known by the name of the Pilgrims' Rest. The history of Hollingbourne is full of interest. The manor was granted to the church at Canterbury, "for the support of the monks," by young Athelstan, the son of Æthelred II., in the year 980, and was retained by the monastery when Lanfranc divided the lands belonging to Christ Church between the priory and the see. It is described in Domesday as *Terra Monachorum Archiepi*, the land of the monk and the Archbishop; in later records as *Manorium Monachorum et de cibo eorum*, a manor of the monks and for their food. The Priors of Christ Church held their courts here, and the convent records tell us that Prior William Sellyng greatly improved the Priory rooms at Hollingbourne. Their residence probably occupied the site of the present manor-house. This handsome red-brick building, rich in gables and mullions, in oak panelling and secret hiding-places, was built in Queen Elizabeth's reign by the great Kentish family of the Culpepers, who at that time owned most of the parish. More than one fragment of the earlier house, encased in the Elizabethan building, has been brought to light, and a pointed stone archway of the thirteenth

57

century, and an old fireplace with herring-bone brickwork, have lately been discovered. Many are the interesting traditions which belong to this delightful old manor-house. The yews in the garden are said to have been planted by Queen Elizabeth on one of her royal progresses through Kent, when she stayed at Leeds Castle, and was the guest of Sir Henry Wotton at Boughton Malherbe. According to another very old local tradition, Katherine Howard, whose mother was a Culpeper, spent some years here as a girl, and the ghost of that unhappy queen is said to haunt one of the upper chambers of the house. Another room, called the Needle-Room, was occupied during the Commonwealth by the daughters of that faithful loyalist, John Lord Culpeper, Frances, Judith, and Philippa, who employed the weary years of their father's exile in embroidering a gorgeous altar-cloth and hangings, which they presented to the parish church on the happy day when the king came back to enjoy his own again. The tapestries, worked by the same deft fingers, which once adorned the chambers of the manor-house, are gone, and the hangings of the reading-desk in the church have been cut up into a frontal, but the altar-cloth remains absolutely intact, and is one of the finest pieces of embroidery of the kind in England. Both design and colouring are of the highest beauty. On a ground of violet velvet, bordered with a frieze of cherub heads, we see the twelve mystic fruits of the Tree of Life—the grape, orange, cherry, apple, plum, pear, mulberry, acorn, peach, medlar, quince, and pomegranate. The richest hues of rose and green are delicately blended together, and their effect is heightened by the gold thread in which the shading is worked. The lapse of two centuries and a half has not dimmed the brightness of their colours, which are as fresh as if the work had been finished yesterday. A needle which had been left in a corner of the altar-cloth all those long years ago was still to be seen sticking in the velvet early in the last century, but has now disappeared.

This goodly manor-house was only one of several seats belonging to the Culpepers in this neighbourhood. They had a mansion at Greenway Court, which was burnt down in the last century, and another of imposing dimensions where Grove Court now stands. In the seventeenth century the Lords Culpeper also owned Leeds Castle, that noble moated house, a mile to the south, which was once a royal park, and is still one of the finest places in Kent. But the second Lord Culpeper died without a male heir in 1688, and this famous house passed by marriage into the Fairfax family. The Hollingbourne branch of the Culpepers died out in the course of the last century, and at the present time no member of this illustrious family is known to exist in England, although persons bearing this ancient name are still to be found in America. The church at Hollingbourne contains a whole series of Culpeper monuments. The most remarkable is the white marble altar-tomb, which bears the recumbent effigy of Elizabeth Lady Culpeper, who died in 1638, and is described in the inscription on her monument as *Optima Fœmina, Optima Conjux, et Optima Mater*. This lady was the heiress of the Cheney family, whose arms, the ox's hide and horns, appear on the shield at the foot of the tomb, and are repeated in the stained glass of the chapel window. Tradition says that Sir John Cheney had his helmet struck off, when he fought by the victor's side on Bosworth Field, and fixed a bull's horns on his head in its place. Afterwards Henry VII. gave him this crest, when he made him a Baron and a Knight of the Garter, in reward for his valour on that hard-fought field. A monument on the north wall of the chancel records the memory of John Lord Culpeper, who was successively Chancellor of the Exchequer, Master of the Rolls, and Privy Councillor to Charles I. and Charles II. "For equal fidelity to the king and kingdome," says the epitaph on his tomb, "he was most exemplary." He followed the last-named king into exile and remained there until the Restoration, when "with him he returned tryumphant into England on the 29th of May, 1660," only to die six weeks afterwards, "to the irreparable losse of his family." Another descendant of the Culpepers is buried under the altar in this church, Dame Grace Gethin, a great grand-daughter of Sir Thomas Culpeper, and wife of Sir Richard Gethin, of Gethinge Grott, in Ireland, whose learning and virtues were so renowned that monuments were erected in her honour both at Bath and in Westminster Abbey. This youthful prodigy, who died at the age of twenty-one, is here represented kneeling between two angels, and holding in her hand the commonplace book which she filled with extracts from her favourite authors, and which was afterwards published under the title of "Reliquiæ Gethinianæ." Her piety was as great as her personal charms, and the inscription on her monument records how, "being adorned with all the Graces and Perfections of mind and body, crowned them all with exemplary Patience and Humility, and having the day before her death most devoutly received the Holy Communion, which she said she would not have omitted for Ten Thousand Worlds, she was vouchsafed in a miraculous manner an immediate prospect of her future Blisse, for the space of two hours, to the astonishment of all about her, and being, like St. Paul, in an unexpressible Transport of joy, thereby fully evincing her foresight of the Heavenly Glory, in unconceivable Raptures triumphing over Death, and continuing sensible to the last, she resigned her pious soul to God, and victoriously entered into rest, Oct. 11th, anno ætatis 21, D'ni: 1697. Her dear and affectionate Mother, whom God in mercy supported by seeing her glorious end, erected this monument, she being her last surviving issue."

Soon after leaving Hollingbourne, the Pilgrims' Way enters the grounds of Stede Hill, and passes through the beech-woods that spread down the grassy slopes to the village and church of Harrietsham—Heriard's Home in Domesday—in the valley below. An altar-tomb, to the memory of Sir William Stede, who died in 1574, and several other monuments to members of the same family, may be seen in the south chapel of the church, a fine building of Early English and Perpendicular work, with a good rood-screen, standing in an open space at the foot of the Stede Hill grounds. The rectory of Harrietsham was formerly attached to the neighbouring Priory of Leeds, but was granted by Henry VI. to Archbishop Chichele's newly founded College of All Souls, Oxford, which still retains the patronage of this living. The manor was one of many in this neighbourhood given to Odo of Bayeux after the battle of Hastings, and afterwards formed part of the vast estates owned by Juliana de Leyborne, called the Infanta of Kent, who was married three times, but died without children, leaving her lands to become crown property.

A mile farther the Pilgrims' Way enters the town of Lenham. This parish contains both the sources of the river Len—the *Aqua lena* of the Romans—which flows through Harrietsham and by Leeds Castle into the Medway, and that of the Stour, which runs in the opposite direction towards Canterbury. Lenham has held a charter, and enjoyed the privileges of a town from mediæval times. The bright little market-square, full of old houses with massive oak beams, and quaint corners jutting out in all directions, hardly agrees with Hasted's description of

Lenham as a dull, unfrequented place, where nothing thrives in the barren soil, and the inhabitants, when asked by travellers if this is Lenham, invariably reply, "Ah, sir, poor Lenham!" The picturesqueness of its buildings is undeniable, and its traditions are of the highest antiquity. The manor of Lenham was granted to the Abbey of St. Augustine at Canterbury by Cenulf, king of Mercia, more than a thousand years ago, and in the twelfth century the church was appropriated to the Refectory of St. Augustine; that is to say, the rectorial tithes were made to supply the monks' dinners. Some fragments of the original Norman church still exist, but the greater part of the present structure, the arcade of bays, the fine traceried windows of the aisle, and most of the chancel, belong to the Decorated period, and were rebuilt after the great fire in 1297, when not only the church, but the Abbot's barns and farm buildings were burnt to the ground by an incendiary. So great was the sensation produced by this act of wanton mischief, that Archbishop Winchelsea himself came to Lenham to see the ravages wrought by the fire, and fulminated a severe excommunication against the perpetrators of the wicked deed. The sixteen oak stalls for the monks, and an arched stone sedilia, of the fourteenth century, which served the Abbot for his throne when he visited his Lenham estates, are still to be seen in the chancel. Here, too, is a sepulchral effigy let into the north wall in a curious sideways position, representing a priest in his robes, supposed to be that of Thomas de Apulderfelde, who lived at Lenham in the reign of Edward II., and died in 1327. Both the western tower and the north chancel, dedicated to St. Edmund, and containing tombs of successive lords of East Lenham manor, are Perpendicular in style, and belong to the fourteenth or early part of the fifteenth century. Fragments of the fourteenth-century paintings, with which the walls of the whole church were once adorned, may still be distinguished in places. Among them are the figures of a bishop, probably St. Augustine, and of St. Michael weighing souls, with devils trying to turn the balance in their favour, on one side, and on the other the crowned Virgin throwing her rosary into the scale which holds the souls of the just. The church was dedicated to St. Mary the Virgin, and her image formerly occupied the niche in the timbered porch which, with the old lych-gate, are such fine specimens of fifteenth-century wood-work. The beautiful Jacobean pulpit was given by Anthony Honywood in 1622, and is charmingly carved with festoons of grapes and vine-leaves. The Honywoods also built the almshouses, with carved bargeboards and door-posts, in the street at Lenham, and an inscription in the chancel floor records the memory of that long-lived Dame, Mary Honywood, who before her death in 1620 saw no less than three hundred and sixty-seven of her descendants!

Close to the church are the great tithe barns, built after the fire in the fourteenth century by the Abbots of St. Augustine. The largest measures 157 feet long by 40 feet wide, and, saving the low stone walls, is built entirely of oak from the forests of the Weald. The enormous timbers are as sound and strong to-day as they were six hundred years ago, and for solidity of material and beauty of construction, this Kentish barn deserves to rank among the grandest architectural works of the age. The monks are gone, and the proud Abbey itself has long been laid in ruins, but these buildings give us some idea of the wealth and resources of the great community who were the lords of Lenham during so many centuries. They could afford to lend a kindly ear to the prayer of the poor vicar when he humbly showed the poverty with which he had to contend, and the load of the burden that he had to bear. The Abbot, we are glad to learn, granted his request, and agreed to give him a roof over his head and to allow his two cows to feed with the monks' own herds in the pastures at Lenham, during the months between the feast of St. Philip and St. James and Michaelmas.

CHAPTER XI

CHARING TO GODMERSHAM

FROM Lenham the Pilgrims' Road threads its lonely way along the hill-side, past one or two decayed farmhouses still bearing the name of the great families who once owned these manors—the Selves and the Cobhams; and the view over the level country grows wider, and extends farther to the south and east, until we reach Charing Hill, one of the highest points along this range of downs. The windmill, a few hundred yards above the track, commands a far-spreading view over the valley, stretching from the foot of the ridge to the Quarry Hills, where the towers of Egerton Church stand out on its steep mound above the hazy plains of the Weald. We look down upon Calehill, the home of the Darells for the last five centuries, and across the woods and park of Surrenden Dering, which has been held by the Dering family ever since the days of Earl Godwin, to the churches and villages of the Weald. Beyond a foreground of swelling hill and dale we see the flat expanse of Romney Marsh and Dungeness; and then for the first time we catch a glimpse of a pale blue line of sea—that sea across which Roman and Saxon and Norman all sailed in turn to land upon the Kentish shore. On clear days you can see the Sussex downs in the far horizon beyond the Weald, and near Hastings, the hill of Fairlight rising sharply from the sea. Down in the valley below, the tall tower of Charing Church lifts its head out of a confused mass of red roofs and green trees, with the ivy-grown ruins of the old palace at its feet.

Many are the venerable traditions attached to the churches and villages which we have seen along our road through this pleasant land of Kent, but here is one older and more illustrious than them all. Here we have a record which goes back far beyond the days of Lanfranc and of Athelstan, and even that king of Mercia who gave Lenham to the Abbey of St. Augustine. For Charing, if not actually given, as the old legend says, by Vortigern to the ancient British Church, was at all events among the first lands bestowed on Augustine and his companions by Ethelbert, king of Kent. Saxon historians tell us how that this most ancient possession of the church of Canterbury was seized by Offa, king of Mercia, in 757, but restored again by his successor, Cenulph, in the year 788.

Long before the Conqueror's time, the Archbishops had a house here. In Domesday Book, Charing is styled "proprium manorium archiepiscopi," being reserved by those prelates for their private use, and from those days until the manor was surrendered by Cranmer to Henry VIII. it remained a favourite residence of the Archbishops. In the thirteenth century the Franciscan Archbishop John Peckham dates many letters from his house at Charing, and Stratford, as Dean Hook tells us, was often there, and found consolation in this quiet retreat for the troubles of those stormy days. Chichele, Kemp, and Bourchier were also frequently here. Stratford first obtained the grant of a three days' fair to be held at Charing twice a year, on the festivals of St. George and St. Luke. Leland tells us that Cardinal Morton made great buildings at Charing, and the red and black brickwork still to be seen under the ivy of the farmhouse walls may be ascribed to him, but the great gateway with the chamber and hooded fireplace above, belongs to an earlier period, and was probably the work of Stratford in the fourteenth century. Some of the older stonework is to be found in the stables and cottages now occupying the site of the offices on the west of the court. The chapel, with its pointed arches and large windows, which in Hasted's time stood behind the modern dwelling-house, was taken down eighty years ago, but the great dining-hall, with its massive walls and fine decorated window, still remains standing. This hall, where archbishops sat in state, and kingly guests were feasted; where Henry VII. was royally entertained by Archbishop Warham, on the 24th of March, 1507, and where Henry VIII. stayed with all his train on his way to the Field of Cloth of Gold, is now used as a barn. But in its decay, it must be owned, the old palace is singularly picturesque. The wallflowers grow in golden clusters high up the roofless gables and along the arches of the central gateway; masses of apple-blossom hang over the grey stone walls, and ring-necked doves bask in the sunshine on the richly coloured tiles of the old banqueting-hall.

Close by is the church of Charing, famous in the eyes of mediæval pilgrims for the possession of one hallowed relic, the block on which St. John the Baptist was beheaded, brought back, an old tradition says, by Richard Cœur de Lion from the Holy Land, and given by him to Archbishop Baldwin, when the King paid his devotions at the shrine of St. Thomas. This precious relic went the way of all relics in the sixteenth century, and is not mentioned in the long list of costly vestments and frontals recorded in an inventory of Church property taken at Charing in 1552. But Charing Church is still, in the words of the old chronicler, "a goodly pile." It is cruciform in shape, and contains some traces of Early English work, but it is mostly of later date. The windows are interesting on account of their great variety. There are three narrow lancets, several of Transitional and Perpendicular style, and one large and very remarkable square-headed Decorated window. The chapel of Our Lady, on the south side of the chancel, was built, towards the close of the fifteenth century, by Amy Brent, whose family owned the charming old manor-house of Wickens in this parish. The porch and fine tower, which forms so marked a feature in the landscape, was also chiefly built by the Brents, whose crest, a wyvern, is carved on the doorway, together with a rose encircled with sun-rays, the badge of Edward IV., in whose reign the work was completed. Through this handsome doorway the Archbishop, attended by his cross-bearers and chaplains, would enter from the palace-gate hard by, and many must have been the stately processions which passed under the western arch and wound up the long nave in the days of Morton and of Warham. A hundred years later Charing Church narrowly escaped entire destruction. On the 4th of August, 1590, a farmer, one Mr. Dios, discharged a birding-piece at a pigeon roosting, as the pigeons do to this day, in the church tower, and "the day being extreme hot and the shingle very dry," a fire broke out in the night, and by morning nothing was left but the bare walls of the church, even the bells being melted by the heat of the fire. Happily the parishioners applied themselves with patriotic zeal to the restoration, and within two years the fine timber roof of the nave was completed. The date 1592, E.R. 34, is inscribed on the rafter above the chancel arch, while that of the chancel roof Ann. Dom. 1622, Anno Regni Jacobi xviii., appears on the beam immediately over the altar.

The Pilgrims' Way winds on through Charing past the noble church tower and the ancient palace wall, with its thick clusters of ivy and trailing wreaths of travellers' joy, through the lovely woods of Pett Place, the home of Honywoods and Sayers for some hundreds of years. The track crosses the long avenue of stately limes which leads up to its gates, and through the meeting boughs we see the red gables and tall chimneys of the old Tudor house. In the fourteenth century the owners of Pett had a chapel of their own, served by a priest whose name appears in the Lambeth Register and other records as holding the living of Pette-juxta-Charing; and Geoffery de Newcourt, who owned this manor, together with the adjoining one of Newcourt, paid the king an aid on his lands of Pett, when the Black Prince was knighted. A pleasant part of the track this is dear to botanists for the wealth of ferns, flowers, and rare orchises which grow along the shady path; pleasant alike in May, when cowslips and violets grow thick in the grass and the nightingales are in full song, and in June, when the ripe red fruit of the wild strawberries peep out from under the moss and the hawthorns are in bloom, but perhaps best of all in autumn, when the beeches are crimson and the maples in the hedges are one fire of gold.

For the next three miles, the way lies through the lower part of the great woods of Long Beech, which stretch all over these hills, and which from very early times belonged to the see of Canterbury. It brings us out at Westwell, close to another extremely interesting church, dating from the middle of the thirteenth century, and almost entirely of one period. The graceful steeple, nave, chancel, and aisles, are all Early English, but the most striking feature is the high open colonnade which forms the rood-screen. The effect of the chancel, with its side arcade, its groined roof, and beautiful lancet window filled with richly-coloured old glass, seen through these three lofty arches, is very imposing. There is another curious fragment of stained glass, bearing the arms of Queen Anne of Bohemia and of Edward the Confessor and his wife, in the north aisle, and the chancel contains six stone walls and a stone seat with a pointed arch, which were formerly used by the monks and prior of Christ Church, Canterbury. For the manor of Westwell, like so many others in this neighbourhood, belonged to the see of Canterbury before the Conquest, and at the division of property effected by Lanfranc was retained by the Priory. Its revenues were allotted to the supply of the monks' refectory, *ad cibum eorum*, just as the tithes of Lenham were used to provide meals for St. Augustine's Abbey.

Half a mile above Westwell Church the Pilgrims' Way reaches the gates of Eastwell. Here the track disappears for a time, but old maps show the line which it took across the southern slopes of the park, which extends for many miles, and is famous for the wild beauty of its scenery. The hills we have followed so long run through the upper part of the park, and magnificent are the views of the sea and Sussex downs which meet us in these forest glades, where stately avenues of beech and oak and chestnut throw long shadows over the grass, and antlered deer start up from the bracken at our feet. But the lower slopes are pleasant too, with the venerable yews and thorns and hornbeams dotted over the hill-side, and the heights above clad with a wealth of mingled foliage which is reflected in the bright waters of the still, clear lake. The old ivy-grown church stands close to the water's edge, and contains some fine tombs of the Earls of Winchelsea, and of their ancestors, the Finches. But the traveller will look with more interest on the sepulchral arch which is said to cover the ashes of the last of the Plantagenets. The burial registers indeed record that Richard Plantagenet, the illegitimate son of Richard III., died at Eastwell on the 22nd of December, 1550, and a well, which goes by the name of Plantagenet's Well, marks the site of the cottage where he lived in confinement after the defeat of his father on Bosworth Field. Eastwell House, for some years the residence of H.R.H. the Duke of Edinburgh, was originally built by Sir Thomas Moyle, Speaker of the House of Commons in the reign of Henry VIII., but has been completely altered and modernised since it passed into the Winchelsea family. Leaving it on our left, we come out of the Park at Boughton Lees, a group of houses on a three-cornered green, and follow in the steps of the old track to Boughton Aluph church, a large cruciform building with a spacious north aisle and massive central tower, standing in a very lonely situation.

Boughton, called Bocton or Boltune in former times, belonged to Earl Godwin and his son Harold, before the Conquest, after which it was given to Eustace, Earl of Boulogne, and formed part of Juliana de Leybourne's vast inheritance. It took the name of Aluph from a Norman knight, Aluphus de Bocton, who held the manor in the reign of King John, and became thus distinguished from the other parishes of Boughton in the neighbourhood. From the church a grassy lane, shaded by trees, ascends the hill to Challock on the borders of Eastwell Park, and is probably the old track of the Pilgrims' Way which passed between these woods and the park of Godmersham. This was formerly the property of Jane Austen's brother, who took the name of Knight on succeeding to the estate, but it has now passed into the hands of another family. Until the Dissolution the manor and church of Godmersham belonged to Christ Church, and here, in mediæval days, the priors of the convent had a fine manor-house, where they frequently resided during the summer months. The hall was pulled down in 1810, and nothing of the old house is now left except a gable and doorway, adorned with a figure of a Prior wearing his mitre and holding his crozier in his hand, probably intended for Henry de Estria, the Prior who rebuilt the manor-house in 1290. The church of Godmersham is remarkable for its early tower and curious semicircular apse with small Norman lights, which are evidently remains of an older building, and in the churchyard are some very ancient yews, one of which is said to have been planted before the Conquest.

Under the shadow of these venerable trees there sleeps a remarkable woman, Mary Sybilla Holland, whose father was at one time Vicar of Godmersham, and afterwards moved to Harbledown, a larger parish near Canterbury, a few miles further along the Pilgrims' Way. Both Mrs. Holland and her distinguished brother, the lamented Sir Alfred Lyall, retained a lifelong affection for this corner of East Kent. When Lyall was far away in India, ruling over millions of British subjects, in the north-west provinces, his verses tell us how passionately he yearned for his old Kentish home.

"Ah! that hamlet in Saxon Kent,
Shall I find it when I come home?
With toil and travelling well-nigh spent,
Tired with life in jungle and tent,
Eastward never again to roam.
Pleasantest corner the world can show
In a vale which slopes to the English sea—
Where strawberries wild in the woodland grow,
And the cherry-tree branches are bending low,
No such fruit in the South countree."

Sir Alfred died on the 10th of April, 1911, at Lord Tennyson's house at Farringford, in the Isle of Wight, and was buried in the churchyard of St. Michael's, Harbledown. Now brother and sister are both sleeping under the grassy sod of the Kentish land which they loved so well, "where the nightingales sing heart-piercing notes in the silence of the early summer night."

"Shelter for me and for you, my friend,
There let us settle when both are old,
And whenever I come to my journey's end,
There you shall see me laid, and blend
Just one tear with the falling mould."

CHAPTER XII

CHILHAM TO HARBLEDOWN

THE Pilgrims' Way skirted the wooded slopes of Godmersham Park for about a mile, and then entered Chilham Park. The park is now closed, but the old track lay right across the park, and in front of Chilham Castle. The position of this fortress, overlooking the valley of the Stour, has made it memorable in English history. Chilham has been in turn a Roman camp, a Saxon castle, and a Norman keep, and has played an eventful part in some of the fiercest struggles of those days. According to a generally received tradition recorded by Camden, Chilham was the scene of the battle on the river in Cæsar's second expedition; and the British barrow near the Stour, popularly known as Julaber's Grave, was believed to be the tomb of the Roman tribune, Julius Laberius, although, as a matter of fact, it contains no sepulchral remains. In the second century Chilham is said to have been the home of that traditional personage, the Christian King Lucius, and in Saxon days of the chief Cilla. The castle was strongly fortified to resist the invasion of the Danes, by whom it was repeatedly attacked. After the Norman Conquest it belonged to Fulbert de Dover, whose last descendant, Isabel, Countess of Atholl, died here in 1292, and is buried in the under-croft at Canterbury. Then it passed into the hands of the great Lord Badlesmere, of Leeds, who on one occasion gave Queen Isabel, the wife of Edward II., a splendid reception here, and afterwards astonished the peaceful citizens and monks of Canterbury by appearing at their gates, followed by nineteen armed knights, each with a drawn sword in his hand, to pay his devotions at the shrine of St. Thomas. As late as the sixteenth century Leland describes Chilham Castle as beautiful for pleasure, commodious for use, and strong for defence; but soon after he wrote these words, the greater part of the old house was pulled down by its owner, Sir Thomas Cheney, Warden of the Cinque Ports under Edward VI., to complete his new mansion in the Isle of Sheppey. The Norman keep, an octagonal fortress three stories high, is the only part of the mediæval structure that now remains, and can still be seen in the gardens of the new house built in 1616 by Sir Dudley Digges, Master of the Rolls in the reign of James I. This fine Jacobean manor-house stands well on the rising ground above the river, and both the garden terrace and the top of the old keep afford beautiful views of the vale of Ashford and the downs beyond the Wye. Still more picturesque is the market-place of Chilham itself. On one side we have the red brick walls and white stone doorway of the castle, seen at the end of its short avenue of tall lime trees on the other the quaint red roofs and timbered houses of the charming old square, with the grey church tower surrounded by the brilliant green of sycamores and beeches. On a bright spring morning, when the leaves are young and the meadows along the river-side are golden with buttercups, there can be no prettier picture than this of the old market square of Cilla's home.

From the heights of Chilham the Pilgrims' Way descends into the valley of the Stour, and after following the course of the river for a short time, climbs the opposite hill and strikes into Bigberry Wood. Here we come suddenly upon the most ancient earthwork along the whole line of the road, an entrenchment which Professor Boyd Dawkins, who explored it thoroughly some years ago, has ascribed to the prehistoric Iron Age. For most of us, perhaps, Bigberry Camp has a still greater interest as the fort which the Britons held against the assault of the Roman invaders, and which was stormed and carried by Cæsar's legions. The memory of that desperate fight, which sealed the fate of Britain and her conquest by the great Proconsul, still lingers in the popular mind, and the shepherd who follows his flock and the waggoner who drives his team along the road, still talk of the famous battle that was fought here two thousand years ago.

After this the path crosses the valley and runs through the hop-gardens to join Watling Street—the road by which Chaucer's pilgrims came to

Canterbury—at Harbledown. This is the little village on the edge of the forest of Blean, which has been immortalised by Chaucer's lines—

"Wist ye not where standeth a little toun
Which that ycleped is Bob-up-and-down,
Under the Blee in Canterbury way."

And Bob-up-and-down is to this day a true and characteristic description of the rolling ground by which we approach Harbledown. Here the Pilgrims' Road, along which we have journeyed over hill and dale, fails to rise again. We climb the last hill, and on the summit of the rising ground we find ourselves close to the lazar-house founded at Harbledown by Lanfranc in 1084. The wooden houses built by the Norman Archbishop for the reception of ten brothers and seven sisters have been replaced by a row of modern almshouses; but the chapel still preserves its old Norman doorway, and the round arches and pillars of an arcade to the north of the nave, which formed part of the hospital church dedicated by Lanfranc to St. Nicholas. The devout pilgrim to St. Thomas's shrine never failed to visit this ancient leper-house. Not only did the antiquity of the charitable foundation and its nearness to the road attract him, but in the common hall of the hospital a precious relic was preserved in the shape of a crystal which had once adorned the leather of St. Thomas's shoe. Many were the royal personages and distinguished strangers who paused before these old walls and dropped their alms into the poor leper's outstretched hand. Here, we read in contemporary records, Henry II. came on his first memorable pilgrimage to the tomb of the martyred Archbishop, and Richard Cœur de Lion after his release from his long captivity. Edward I. stopped at Harbledown with his brave Queen, Eleanor of Castille, on their return from the Holy Land, and the Black Prince, accompanied by his royal captive, King John of France, and that monarch's young son Philip, also visited the leper-house. And when the French king visited Canterbury for the second time, on his return to his own kingdom, he did not forget to stop at Lanfranc's old lazar-house and leave ten gold crowns "pour les nonnains de Harbledoun." But it is a later and more sceptical traveller, Erasmus, who has left us the most vivid description of Harbledown and of the feelings which the sight of the relic aroused in the heart of his companion, Dean

Colet. "Not far from Canterbury, at the left-hand side of the road," he writes, in the record of his pilgrimage, "there is a small almshouse for old people, one of whom ran out, seeming to hear the steps of the horses. He first sprinkled us with holy water, and then offered us the upper leather of a shoe bound in a brass rim, with a crystal set in its centre like a jewel. Gration (Dean Colet) rode on my left hand, nearer to the beggar man, and was duly sprinkled, bearing it with a tolerable amount of equanimity. But when the shoe was handed up, he asked the old man what he wanted. 'It is the shoe of St. Thomas,' was the answer. Upon this he fired up, and turning to me, exclaimed indignantly, 'What! do these cattle mean we should kiss the shoes of every good man?'" Erasmus, sorry for the old man's feelings, dropped a small coin into his hand, which made him quite happy, and the two pilgrims rode on to London, discussing the question of the worship of relics as they went. To this day a maple bowl, bound with a brass rim, containing a piece of crystal, is preserved in the hospital at Harbledown, the self-same relic, it may be, which was shown to Erasmus and Colet, and which Lambarde, writing half a century later, describes as "faire set in copper and chrystall"; while an old wooden box, with a slit in the lid for money, and a chain attached to it, is said to be the one into which Erasmus dropped his coin.

Behind the ivy-mantled tower of Lanfranc's chapel is a clear spring which was supposed to possess healing virtues, and is still believed by the country folks to be of great benefit to the eyes. This spring still goes by the name of the Black Prince's Well, from an old tradition that the warrior of Crecy and Poitiers drank of its waters when he visited the hospital at Harbledown in 1357. Many, we know, are the memorials of this popular hero at Canterbury. Only three days after he landed at Sandwich he came, accompanied by his royal captive, to return thanks at St. Thomas's shrine for his victories, and six years afterwards he founded and decorated the beautiful chantry in the Cathedral crypt, which still bears his name, on the occasion of his marriage with his cousin Joan, the Fair Maid of Kent. The old legend of the Black Prince's Well goes on to tell how, when he lay dying of the wasting disease which carried him off in the flower of his life, he thought of the wonder-working spring near Canterbury, and sent to Harbledown for a draught of its pure waters. But even that could not save him, and on the 29th of September, 1376, a stately funeral procession wound its way down the hill-side at Harbledown, bearing the Black Prince to the grave which he had chosen for himself in the Chapel of Our Lady of the Undercroft at Canterbury.

At Harbledown the pilgrims caught their first sight of the Cathedral; here they fell on their knees when they saw the golden angel on the top of the central tower, and knew that the goal of their pilgrimage was almost reached. Here Chaucer's goodly company made their last halt, and for the moment the noise of singing and piping and jingling of bells gave place to a graver and more solemn mood as the motley crowd of pilgrims pressed around, to hear this time not a Canterbury tale, but a sermon. Deep was the impression which that first sight of Canterbury made upon Erasmus. The cold, critical scholar becomes eloquent as he describes the great church of St. Thomas rearing itself up into the sky with a majesty that strikes awe into every heart, and the clanging of bells which, thrilling through the air, salute the pilgrims from afar. To-day the great cross is gone from the Westgate, the shining archangel no longer blesses the kneeling pilgrim from the topmost steeple, but the same glorious vision of the great Cathedral rising with all its towers into the sky meets the eyes of the traveller who looks down on Canterbury from the hill of Harbledown.

CHAPTER XIII

HARBLEDOWN TO CANTERBURY

FROM Harbledown it is all downhill to Canterbury, and a short mile brings us to the massive round tower of Simon of Sudbury's noble Westgate, the only one remaining of the seven fortified gateways which once guarded the ancient city. Many are the pilgrims who have entered Canterbury by this gate: kings and queens of all ages, foreign emperors and princes, armed knights and humble scholars, good Queen Philippa and Edward Plantagenet, Henry of Agincourt, Margaret of Anjou, Chaucer and Erasmus. Many, too, are the long processions which have wound down this hill-side: newly created archbishops followed by a brilliant train of bishops and courtiers on their way to be enthroned in the chair of St. Augustine; solemn funerals, attended with all the pomp and circumstance, the funeral plumes and sable trappings, with which men honour the mighty dead. Through the Westgate went forth that gay company of monks and friars, of merchants and citizens crowned with garlands of flowers, and making joyous minstrelsy, as they rode out to welcome Archbishop Winchelsea, who, once a poor student in the school at Canterbury, now came to be enthroned in state in the presence of King Edward I. and all his court. And this way, too, they bore him with much state and pomp, eighteen years later, from the manor-house at Otford, where he died, to sleep in his own Cathedral after all the labours and struggles, the storms and changes of his troublous reign.

Since these mediæval days Canterbury has seen many changes. The splendours of which Camden and Leland wrote have passed away, the countless number of its churches has been reduced, and their magnificence no longer strikes the eye of the stranger. The lofty walls and their twenty-one watch-towers, which encircled the city in a complete ring when Chaucer's knight, after paying his devotion at the shrine of St. Thomas, went out to see their strength, and "pointed to his son both the perill and the doubt," are all gone, and the Conqueror's mighty castle is turned into a coal-pit. But the old city is still full of quaint corners and picturesque buildings, timbered houses with carved corbels and oriel windows, hostelries with overhanging eaves and fantastic sign-boards of wrought-iron work, hospitals whose charters date from Norman times, and whose records give us many a curious peep into the byways of mediæval life.

As we draw near the Martyr's shrine, memories of St. Thomas crowd upon us. The hill outside the Westgate, now occupied by the Clergy Orphan School, is still called St. Thomas's Hill, and was formerly the site of a chapel founded by Becket himself. A little way up the High Street we reach a bridge over the Stour, which winds its way through the heart of the city, and a low pointed doorway on our right leads into St. Thomas's Hospital. This ancient Spittle of East Bridge was founded, as a fourteenth-century charter records, by the "glorious St. Thomas the Martyr, to receive poor wayfaring men." Archbishop Hubert Walter increased its endowments in the twelfth century, and Stratford repaired the walls in the fourteenth, and drew up statutes for its government. From that time it was especially devoted to the use of poor pilgrims, for whom twelve beds were provided, and whose wants were supplied at the rate of fourpence a day. During those days, when the enthusiasm for St. Thomas was at its height, alms and legacies were lavished upon Eastbridge Hospital, and Edward III. bequeathed money to support a chaplain, whose duty it was to say daily masses for the founders of the hospital. After the days of pilgrimages were over, this hospital was applied to various uses until Archbishop Whitgift recovered the property and drew up fresh statutes for its management. Ten poor brothers and sisters still enjoy the fruit of St. Thomas's benevolence, and dwell in the old house built on arches across the bed of the river. The low level of the floor, which has sunk far below that of the street, and the vaulted roof and time-worn pillars, bear witness to its great antiquity. There can be little doubt that the round arches of the Norman crypt belong to St. Thomas's original foundation, while the pointed windows of the chapel and Early English arches of the refectory form part of Archbishop Stratford's improvements. In this hall some portions of frescoes, representing on the one hand the Last Supper, on the other the Martyrdom of the Saint, the penance of Henry II. at his tomb, with the central figure of Christ in Glory, have been lately recovered from under the coat of whitewash which had concealed them for more than two centuries.

Twice a year, we know, at the summer festival of the Translation of St. Thomas, on the 7th of July, and at the winter festival of the Martyrdom, on the 29th of December, Canterbury was crowded with pilgrims, and a notice was placed in the High Street ordering the due provision of beds and entertainment for strangers. The concourse was still greater on the jubilees of the Translation, when indulgences were showered freely on all who visited the shrine, and the festival lasted for a whole fortnight. At the jubilee of the year 1420, just after the victory of Agincourt, no less than a hundred thousand pilgrims are said to have been present. On such occasions every available corner was occupied; the inns, which were exceedingly numerous, the hospitals, and, above all, the religious houses, were thronged with strangers. The most favourite, the most renowned, of all the hostelries was the Chequers of the Hope, the inn where Chaucer's twenty-nine pilgrims took up their quarters.

"At Chekers of the Hope that every man doth know."

This ancient inn, which Prior Chillenden rebuilt about 1400, stood at the corner of High Street and Mercery Lane, the old Merceria, which was formerly lined with rows of booths and stalls for the sale of pilgrimage tokens, such as are to be found in the neighbourhood of all famous shrines. Both ampullas, small leaden bottles containing a drop of the martyr's blood, which flowed perennially from a well in the precincts, and Caput Thomæ, or brooches bearing the saint's mitred head, were eagerly sought after by all Canterbury pilgrims. So too were the small metal bells which are said to have given their name to the favourite Kentish flower, the Canterbury bell. And we read that the French king, John, stopped at the Mercery stalls to buy a knife for the Count of Auxerre. The position of the inn close to the great gate of Christ Church naturally attracted many visitors, and the spacious cellars with vaulted roofs, which once belonged to the inn, may still be seen, although the inner courtyard and the great chamber upstairs occupied by the pilgrims, and known as the Dormitory of Hundred Beds, were burnt down forty years ago. But the old street front, with its broad eaves overhanging the narrow lane leading up to the great gateway at the other end, still remains, and renders Mercery Lane the most picturesque and interesting corner of the Cathedral city.

The religious houses were open to all comers, and while royal visitors were lodged in St. Augustine's Abbey, the convents of the Mendicant orders were largely frequented by the poorer classes. There was also the house of the Whitefriars or Augustinians in the eastern part of the town, close to St. George's Gate, and the hospital of St. John in the populous Northgate, "that faire and large house of stone," built and endowed by Lanfranc in the eleventh century, besides that of Eastbridge, which has been already mentioned, and many other smaller foundations.

But it was in the great Priory of Christ Church that by far the largest number of pilgrims found hospitable welcome. A considerable part of the convent buildings was set aside for their reception. The Prior himself entertained distinguished strangers, and lodged them in the splendid suite of rooms overlooking the convent garden, known as the Omers or Homers—Les Ormeaux—from a neighbouring grove of elms. This range of buildings, including the banqueting-hall, generally known as "Meister Omers," was broken up into prebendal houses after the Dissolution, and supplied three separate residences for members of the new Chapter, which gives us some idea of the size of these lodgings. For ordinary strangers there was the Guest Hall, near the kitchen, on the west side of the Prior's Court, which was under the especial charge of a cellarer appointed to provide for the needs of the guests. Prior Chillenden, whom Leland describes as "the greatest builder of a Prior that ever was in Christ Church," repaired and enlarged this Strangers' Hall early in the fifteenth century, and added a new chamber for hospitality, which bore the name of Chillenden's Guest Chamber, and now forms part of the Bishop of Dover's house. Finally, without the convent precincts, close to the court gateway, where the beautiful Norman stairway leads up to the Great Hall, or Aula Nova, was the Almonry. Here the statutes of Archbishop Winchelsea—he who had known what it was to hunger and thirst in his boyhood, and who remained all through his greatness the friend of the poor—provided that poor pilgrims and beggars should be fed daily with the fragments of bread and meat, "which were many and great," left on the monks' tables, and brought here by the wooden pentise or covered passage leading from the kitchen. This Almonry became richly endowed by wealthy pilgrims in course of years, and early in the fourteenth century Prior Henry of Estria built a chapel close by, which was dedicated to St. Thomas the Martyr, and much frequented by pilgrims. The Almony was turned into a mint-yard at the Dissolution, and the chapel and priests' lodgings attached to it, now belong to the King's School. Another privilege freely conceded by the prior and monks of this great community to pilgrims of all ranks and nationality who might die at Canterbury, was that of burial within the precincts of Christ Church, close to the blessed martyr's shrine, and under the shadow of the Cathedral walls.

CHAPTER XIV

THE MARTYR'S SHRINE

ERASMUS has described the imposing effect of the great Cathedral church on the stranger who entered its doors for the first time, and saw the nave "in all its spacious majesty." The vision which broke upon the eyes of those pilgrims who, like himself and Dean Colet, visited Canterbury in the early years of the sixteenth century, may well have filled all hearts with wonder. For then the work was well-nigh perfected. The long roll of master-builders, from Prior Wibert and De Estria to Chillenden and Sellyng, had faithfully accomplished their task. Prior Goldstone, the last but one who reigned before the Dissolution, had just completed the central tower, the great labour of his predecessor Prior Sellyng's life, and was in the act of building the noble Perpendicular gateway which forms a fitting entrance to the precincts.

And now the great church stood complete. Without, "a very goodly, strong, and beautiful structure": the traceries and mouldings of the windows, the stone canopies and sculptured images of the portal, all perfect; the glorious towers in their might; Bell Harry Steeple, as we see it to-day, matchless in its strength and beauty; and beside it, rivalling its grace and majesty, the ancient Norman tower, which bore the name of Ethelbert, crowned with the Arundel spire. Within, a richness and splendour to which our eyes are wholly unaccustomed: chapels and chantries lining the great nave, fresh from Prior Chillenden's work; altars glittering with lighted tapers and gold and silver ornaments; roof and walls bright with painting and gilding, or decked with silken tapestry hangings; carved images covered with pearls and gems; stained windows throwing their hues of ruby and sapphire across the floor, and lighting up the clouds of incense as they rose heavenward. All this, and much more, met the pilgrims' wondering eyes. No wonder they stood "half amazed," as the Supplementary Tale to Chaucer's Pilgrimage describes "the gardener and the miller and the other lewd sets," gazing up at the painted windows, and forgetting to move on with the crowd.

Then the show began. First of all the pilgrims were led up a vaulted passage and "many steps" to the Transept of the Martyrdom, where the wooden altar, at the foot of which the saint fell, remained to show the actual place of the murder, and its guardian priest—the *Custos Martyrum* —displayed the rusty sword of Richard le Breton. Next, descending the flight of steps on the right, they were led into the dark crypt, where more priests received them, and presented the saint's skull, encased in silver, to be kissed, and other relics, including the famous girdle and hair-shirt. This *Caput Thomæ* was one of the chief stations at which offerings were made, and the altar on which it lay, mentioned in the Black Prince's will as "the altar where the head is," marked the site of the original grave where the saint was buried by the frightened monks on the day after the murder. The tomb stood in the eastern chapel of Ernulf's crypt, under the beautiful Pointed arches afterwards raised by that great architect, William the Englishman, whom Gervase describes as "small in body, but in workmanship skilled and honest." Soon it acquired a miraculous virtue, and the fame of the cures and wonders wrought there rang throughout the world. It was the scene of Henry II.'s penance, and during the next fifty years it remained the central object of interest to the crowds of pilgrims who came from all parts of Christendom. Cœur de Lion, accompanied by William, King of Scotland, knelt here on his way to the Crusades, to implore the martyr's blessing on his arms. Many were the Crusaders from all parts of France and England who came thither on the same errand. King John and his wife Isabella, who were crowned at Canterbury Cathedral by Archbishop Hubert Walter, at Easter, 1201, offered their coronation canopies at this tomb and vast sums of money were yearly offered here until 1220, when the body of St. Thomas was translated, in the presence of the young King Henry III., to the new Shrine in Trinity Chapel, immediately above the tomb in the crypt. In that year the offerings at the tomb, at the Altar of the Sword's Point, and at the new Shrine, reached the enormous amount of £1,071, a sum equal to more than £20,000 of money at the present time. After this, the offerings at the original tomb in the crypt diminished in number and value, but the altar and relics of the *Caput Thomæ* remained an object of deep reverence until the Reformation.

From the dark vaults of the subterranean church the pilgrims were led up the steps to the north aisle of the choir. Here the great mass of relics, including St. George's arm and no less than four hundred skulls, jaws, teeth, hands, and other bones, were displayed in gold, silver, or ivory caskets, and pilgrims were allowed a glimpse of the magnificent vessels and ornaments stored up under the high altar. "All the gold of Midas and Crœsus," exclaims Erasmus, "would have been nothing by the side of these treasures!" and he confesses that he sighed to think he kept no such relics at home, and had to beg the saint's pardon for this very unholy emotion. The golden candlesticks and silken vestments of the sacristy in St. Andrew's tower, and the saint's pallium, which no ordinary pilgrims might see, were also shown to Erasmus and Colet, who brought with them a letter of introduction from Archbishop Warham.

After duly inspecting these precious objects, they mounted the long flight of steps behind the high altar leading into Trinity Chapel; a continual ascent, "church, as it were, piled upon church," which seems to have greatly heightened the impression produced upon the awe-struck pilgrims. Now at last they stood within the holiest of holies. There, before their eyes, was the goal of all their journeyings, the object of their deepest devotion, the Shrine which held the body of the blessed martyr.

The Shrine itself, covered by a painted canopy of wood, rested on stone arches in the centre of the floor, exactly under the gilded crescent which is still to be seen in the Cathedral roof. On the right was the richly carved and canopied monument of Henry IV. and his Queen, Joan of Navarre, with its elaborate effigies of the royal pair wearing their crowns and robes of state; on the left the tomb of Edward the Black Prince. He had willed to sleep before the altar of Our Lady of the Under-croft, in the chapel adorned by his own gifts, but the people who had loved him so well would not allow their hero to remain buried out of sight in the dark crypt. So they brought him to rest by the great saint's Shrine, where all men could see his effigy of gilded bronze as he lay there, clad in armour, his sword by his side, his hands clasped in prayer, and read the pathetic lines which tell of his departed glories, and bid the passing stranger pray for his soul:

"Pur Dieu, priez au Celestien Roy,
Que mercy ait de l'âme de moy."

His was the first tomb that was ever raised in the sacred precincts devoted to the martyr's Shrine, and to this day it remains there, unhurt by the hand of time or the more cruel violence of man.

Up the worn stone steps which still bear the marks left by thousands of feet and knees, the pilgrims climbed, murmuring words of prayer or chanting the popular Latin hymns to St. Thomas:

"Tu, per Thomæ sanguinem,
Quem pro te impendit,
Fac nos, Christe, scandere
Quo Thomas ascendit."

Here the Prior himself received them, and showed them first the corona or crown of Becket's head, preserved in a golden likeness of St. Thomas's face, ornamented with pearls and precious gems, which had been presented by Henry V. Then, at a given sign, the wooden canopy was drawn up by ropes, and the Shrine itself, embossed with gold and glittering with countless jewels that flashed and sparkled with light, was revealed to the eyes of the pilgrims. They all fell upon their knees and worshipped, while the Prior with his white wand pointed out the balass-rubies and diamonds, the sapphires and emeralds, which adorned the Shrine, and told the names of the royal persons by whom these gifts had been presented. There were rings and brooches and chains without end, golden and silver statues offered by kings and queens, the crown of Scotland brought back by Edward I. after his victory over John Baliol, and the *regale* of France, that superb ruby presented at the tomb in the crypt by Louis VII., which shone like fire, and was as costly as a king's ransom. Full of awe and wonder the spectators gazed with admiring eyes on these treasures, which for beauty and splendour were beyond all they had ever dreamt, until the canopy slowly descended, and the Shrine was once more hidden from their sight.

Then they went their way, some to visit the convent buildings, the noble chapter-house with its gabled roof and stained windows, and the glazed walk of the cloisters, glowing with bright colours and decorated with heraldic devices of benefactors to Christ Church painted on the bosses of the vaulting. Others made themselves fresh and gay, and went out to see the city, the Knight and his son to look at the walls, the Prioress and the Wife of Bath to walk in the herbary of the inn.

But for Erasmus and his rather inconvenient companion there was still a sight in store, only reserved for very exalted personages, or such as had friends at court. Prior Goldstone, a gentle and well-bred man, not altogether ignorant, as Erasmus found, of the Scotian theology, himself took them back into the crypt, and lanterns were brought to illumine the dark vaults. By their light the Prior led the way into the church of Our Lady of the Undercroft, which was divided from the rest of the crypt by strong iron railings. Here the two friends saw what Erasmus might well call "a display of more than royal splendour." For here, surrounded by exquisitely carved stonework screens and a beautiful reredos with delicate traceries and mouldings, richly coloured and gilt, was the altar of Our Lady, adorned with precious ornaments and twinkling with hundreds of silver lamps. There in the central niche, under a crocketed and pinnacled canopy, stood the famous silver image of the Blessed Virgin herself. And there was the jewelled tabernacle and frontal, with its picture of the Assumption worked in gold, and the chalice and cruets in the form of angels, and the great silver candelabra with which the Black Prince had enriched his favourite shrine. There too were the costly gifts and jewels presented by his son, Richard II., the gold brooches offered yearly by Edward I., the white silk vestments, diapered with a vine pattern of blue, bequeathed by the Black Prince, and countless other rare and precious things, which filled Erasmus with envy and wonder. But then, as ill luck would have it, the Prior conducted his guests into the sacristy, where on bended knees he opened a black leathern chest, out of which he produced a parcel of ragged handkerchiefs with which St. Thomas used to wipe his face. This was too much for Dean Colet's patience, already sorely tried as it had been by what he had seen and heard. When the gentle Prior offered him one of the filthy rags as a present, he shrank back in evident disgust, and turned up his nose with an expression of contempt which filled Erasmus with shame and terror. Fortunately the Prior was a man of sense and courtesy, so he appeared to take no notice, and after giving his guests a cup of wine, politely bade them farewell.

Before this Colet had alarmed his more timid friend by the bold way in which he had dared to question the priest who guarded the gilded head. He had even gone so far as to remark aloud that the saint who was so charitable in his lifetime, would surely be better pleased if some trifling part of these riches were spent in relieving the poor and destitute. Upon which the monk had glared at him with Gorgon eyes, and, Erasmus felt sure, would have turned them out of the church forthwith, had it not been for Archbishop Warham's letter.

But in these words of the honest Dean we see a foreboding of the new and critical spirit that was fast undermining the old beliefs. Already the days of pilgrimages were numbered, and the glories of St. Thomas were on the wane. A few more years and the monks who guarded his treasures were rudely disturbed. The glorious Shrine was stripped of its priceless gems. The wrought gold and precious jewels were borne away in two enormous chests, such as six or seven men could barely lift. The wonderful ruby which flashed fire in the darkness was set in a ring and worn by King Harry himself on his thumb. Finally, to complete the sacrilege, the relics of the Saint were publicly burnt and his ashes scattered to the winds. Only the broken pavement and the marks of the pilgrims' knees in the stone floor were left to show future generations this spot, hallowed by the prayers and the worship of past ages.

Printed in Great Britain
by Amazon

48834539R00051